DIVE DEEP

Pauline
BOOKS & MEDIA
Boston

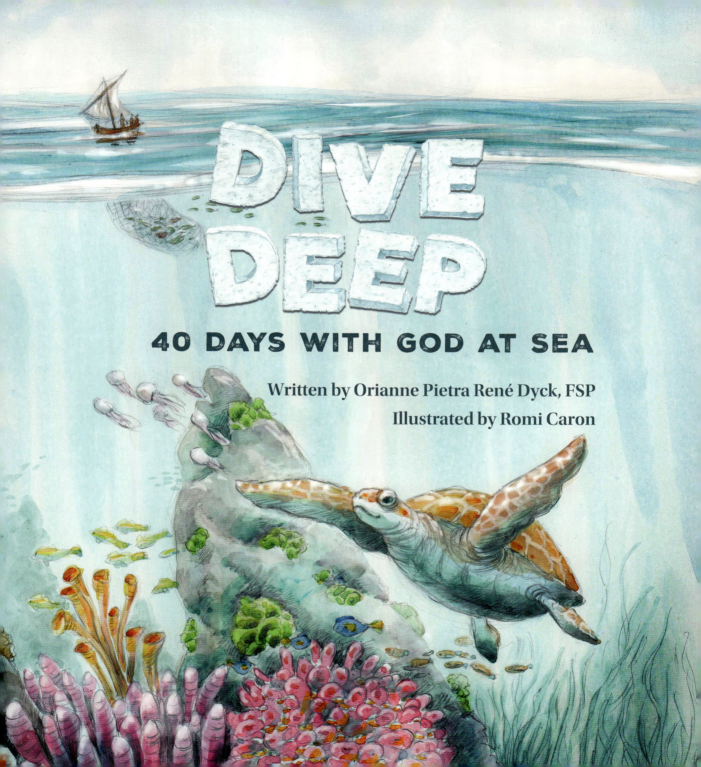

Library of Congress Control Number: 9780819819185

ISBN 10: 0-8198-1918-2
ISBN 13: 978-0-8198-1918-5

Illustrated by Romi Caron

Scripture quotations unless otherwise noted are from *New Revised Standard Version Bible: Catholic Edition*, copyright © 1989, 1993 National Council of the Churches of Christ in the United States of America. Used by permission. All rights reserved worldwide.

Scripture quotation marked (ESV) is from The ESV® Bible (The Holy Bible, English Standard Version®), copyright © 2001 by Crossway, a publishing ministry of Good News Publishers. Used by permission. All rights reserved.

All rights reserved. No part of this book may be reproduced or transmitted in any form or by any means, electronic or mechanical, including photocopying, recording, or by any information storage and retrieval system, without permission in writing from the publisher.

Extracts from papal documents copyright © Dicastero per la Comunicazione-Libreria Editrice Vaticana.

"P" and PAULINE are registered trademarks of the Daughters of St. Paul.

Copyright © 2024, Daughters of Saint Paul

Published by Pauline Books & Media, 50 Saint Paul's Avenue, Boston, MA 02130-3491

Printed in Korea.

DD40DWGAS SIPSKOGUNKYO4-290991918-2

www.pauline.org

Pauline Books & Media is the publishing house of the Daughters of St. Paul, an international congregation of women religious serving the Church with the communications media.

1 2 3 4 5 6 7 8 9   29 28 27 26 25 24

For my goddaughter, Isabel.
May you have many great adventures with Jesus!

Sea *noun* 1. the salt water that covers most of the earth, as opposed to the land and the air; 2. salt water mostly surrounded by land, but connected to the ocean, such as the Caribbean Sea; 3. ocean; 4. a large body of water that is landlocked, a large lake, such as the Caspian Sea

Contents

Charting the Course 1

PART ONE
OLD TESTAMENT

CREATION 4
    Day 1: Setting Sail 6
    Day 2: Deep Dive 10

NOAH 12
    Day 3: Setting Sail 14
    Day 4: Deep Dive 17

GOD'S PROMISE TO ABRAHAM 20
    Day 5: Setting Sail 22
    Day 6: Deep Dive 25

MOSES PARTS THE RED SEA 28
    Day 7: Setting Sail 30
    Day 8: Deep Dive 33

LEVIATHAN 36
   Day 9: Setting Sail 38
   Day 10: Deep Dive 41

JONAH 44
   Day 11: Setting Sail 46
   Day 12: Deep Dive 48

DANIEL 50
   Day 13: Setting Sail 52
   Day 14: Deep Dive 55

PART TWO
NEW TESTAMENT

MIRACULOUS CATCH 60
   Day 15: Setting Sail 62
   Day 16: Deep Dive 65

CALLING FISHERMEN 69
   Day 17: Setting Sail 70
   Day 18: Deep Dive 74

AFTER JOHN THE BAPTIST DIES 76
    Day 19: Setting Sail 78
    Day 20: Deep Dive 81

JESUS AND PETER WALK ON WATER 84
    Day 21: Setting Sail 86
    Day 22: Deep Dive 89

JESUS ASLEEP IN THE BOAT 92
    Day 23 Setting Sail 94
    Day 24: Deep Dive 97

JESUS GETS FRUSTRATED 101
    Day 25: Setting Sail 102
    Day 26: Deep Dive 105

HAIL, OUR ONLY HOPE 108

AFTER THE RESURRECTION: SEA OF TIBERIUS 110
    Day 27: Setting Sail 112
    Day 28: Deep Dive 115

ACTS OF THE APOSTLES: PAUL'S SHIPWRECK 118
    Day 29: Setting Sail 120
    Day 30: Deep Dive 123

REVELATION: GOLDEN CROWNS 126

    Day 31: Setting Sail 128

    Day 32: Deep Dive 131

PART THREE
THE CHURCH

    Day 33: Stella Maris: Mary 136

    Day 34: Saint Brendan 139

    Day 35: Saint Francis Xavier 143

    Day 36: Saint Lorenzo Ruiz 146

    Day 37: Saint Marguerite Bourgeoys . . 150

    Day 38: Saint Damien of Molokai . . . 153

    Day 39: Saint Josephine Bakhita 156

    Day 40: My Story 159

Safe at Port 162

How to Look Up a Passage in the Bible . . . 163

How Catholics Understand the Bible . . . 164

Prayers Before Reading the Bible 166

For Further Exploration:
    Notes for Individual Days 167

Charting the Course

Dear Reader,

You are about to cross many seas and meet people from thousands of years of human history who were seeking the heart of God. As you join them in their experiences at sea, we pray that you will find yourself encountering that same God.

The Bible, or Sacred Scripture, is a very special gift to us, because it is the word of God. Over hundreds of years, the Holy Spirit inspired authors from all walks of life to share specific stories, memories, historical accounts, or personal experiences. The Holy Spirit did this so that, together, all the words of these authors would reveal to us the truth of who God is! As Scripture says in Hebrews 4:12, "the word of God is living and active, sharper than any two-edged sword. . . ." The word of God doesn't get dull over time—it stays sharp. Since the word of God is living, God always has something new to tell us through it.

Bible stories tell us different kinds of things. First, each story of the Bible tells us about experiences of God and his people in their journey together. When we look at all the stories together, we can see God working through everybody's lives!

Some stories show us what not to do, such as say horrible things or make bad decisions. Other stories show us people full of courage who tried to do what was good. In them we develop "best friends" in the Bible, people that we relate to or who inspire us.

God can also use each story to speak directly to us. He can answer our questions by showing us how he helped someone going through a situation like ours. Or he can use a piece of a story to give us a new idea. God can use one story to tell us several different things, as you will see in this devotional. For each Bible story, you will pray with two very different things that God reveals to us through it. So read each Bible story very carefully and refer back to the stories as you pray with the reflection of that day. Some of the longer Bible stories are abbreviated to fit the pages of this devotional. We kept in all the important bits, but if you'd like to pray with the full story, open up a Bible and find the right passage. (Use the citations included under the story's title, and the instructions on page 163.) Some days have material for further exploration, which you can find on page 167.

May you have fair winds and following seas!

Part One
OLD TESTAMENT

It is our duty to thank the Creator for the impressive and marvellous gift of the great waters and all that they contain.

—Pope Francis, Fourth World Day of Prayer for the Care of Creation

God creates the earth and the first man and woman. Because he loves them, he gives them free will. With free will, they can choose to love God and one another. But when these first human beings choose to say no to God's love, they break their close friendship with God. They were meant to pass on to their descendants a whole and deep bond with God. They were meant to be stewards of creation. But now their sin is passed down to their descendants, and it also affects the whole world. But God won't abandon his people to their sin. He will give everything to save his people. Over many generations, he starts to prepare them, slowly but surely, to accept the Messiah that he is going to send to save them from their sins.

Creation

In the beginning when God created the heavens and the earth, the earth was a formless void and darkness covered the face of the deep, while a wind from God swept over the face of the waters. Then God said, "Let there be light"; and there was light. . . . God called the light Day, and the darkness he called Night. . . .

And God said, "Let there be a dome in the midst of the waters, and let it separate the waters from the waters." So God made the dome and separated the waters that were under the dome from the waters that were above the dome. And it was so. God called the dome Sky. . . .

And God said, "Let the waters under the sky be gathered together into one place, and let the dry land appear." And it was so. God called the dry land Earth, and the waters that were gathered together he called Seas. And God saw that it was good . . . .

And God said, "Let there be lights in the dome of the sky to separate the day from the night; and let them be for signs and for seasons and for days and years, and let them be lights in the dome of the sky to give light upon the earth." And it was so. God made the two great lights—the greater light to rule the day and the lesser light to rule the night—and the stars. . . . And God saw that it was good. . . .

And God said, "Let the waters bring forth swarms of living creatures, and let birds fly above the earth across the dome of the sky." So God created the great sea monsters and every living creature that moves, of every kind, with which the waters swarm, and every

winged bird of every kind. And God saw that it was good. God blessed them, saying, "Be fruitful and multiply and fill the waters in the seas, and let birds multiply on the earth...."

Then God said, "Let us make humankind in our image, according to our likeness; and let them have dominion over the fish of the sea, and over the birds of the air, and over the cattle, and over all the wild animals of the earth, and over every creeping thing that creeps upon the earth."

So God created humankind in his image,
    in the image of God he created them;
    male and female he created them.

God blessed them, and God said to them, "Be fruitful and multiply, and fill the earth and subdue it; and have dominion over the fish of the sea and over the birds of the air and over every living thing that moves upon the earth...." God saw everything that he had made, and indeed, it was very good.

Genesis 1:1–3, 5, 6–8, 9–10, 14–16, 18, 20–22, 26–28, 31

DAY 1
Setting Sail

Did you know that there are actually two different creation stories in Genesis? And they're not the same! They give different takes on when God created what, and how. That might seem confusing, but these two stories aren't meant to be scientific records. We aren't supposed to read them that way. They are stories that God inspired to help us understand real truths from the beginning of time, long before people had developed systems of reading or writing. So they aren't totally literal accounts. But that doesn't mean they aren't true. They do tell us important truths that we need for understanding ourselves and God.

Did you notice that in this first creation story, water was one of the first things created? The seas were basins of life, where all sorts of species came to be. Did you also notice that in this story, humans were created last? That doesn't mean that *Homo sapiens* were the last species of creature that ever came to be. Both scientific research and the second creation story in Genesis show that humans weren't the last species to ever develop. But in the first creation story, the creation of humans at the end does teach us that human beings were the peak of God's creation. And it reminds us that we didn't see how God did most of the creating—we have to explore the world to discover many of these things.

When God created the waters, he created what Scripture calls "swarms" of living creatures—basically, A LOT. All these years later, humans still haven't discovered them all! We have very little idea of just what the sea is like in its deepest places, or what might be down there.

FACT: We actually have better maps of the surface of Mars than we do of most of the ocean floor! Even after hundreds of years of research and advances in modern technology, most of the ocean remains a complete mystery.

There is ALWAYS more to learn about the ocean, always more to discover, and always more to love. Just as there is with God. Sometimes it feels like getting to know God is hard. Even though God is always near, he really can be a mystery. Other times we may feel like we know everything about him. But just when we think we have figured out exactly who he is and how he acts, we discover more! God is infinite—there is always more to get to know about his heart. There is always more to discover. There is always more to love.

What is your experience of God? Do you feel like you've never really met God? Like you've heard *about* him, but don't really *know* him yourself. . . . Or do you feel like you know God pretty well? Like you've been talking to him for years? Wherever you are at in your life's walk with God, these forty days will help you encounter him in a new way in your life. Getting to know God won't end on Day 40. God is vast enough for you to keep discovering amazing new things for the rest of your life and beyond!

 Prayer Prompt

Lord, you know me and love me so well, but I am still getting to know you. I am excited to get to know you better. Please help me to notice you around me today.

 Sailor's Log

What are three things that you already know or have heard about God? Note them with bullet points or illustrations:

DAY 2

Deep Dive

God tells the first humans that they will "have dominion" over all the creatures (that is, that they are responsible for the creatures). First on the list are "the fish of the sea." Have you ever wondered why God trusts us to care for something that is so hard for us to even see? Fish live underwater, exactly where we can't survive, so finding them and caring for them is tricky. Even if we stand by the sea, we probably won't see a fish right away—it takes careful searching and observation for us to spot one. But God still asks us to take responsibility for them.

Fish aren't the only thing we might have trouble seeing. We might have trouble seeing God, too. It isn't always easy for us to see God working in our lives—it takes searching and observation. And yet, he calls us to enter into relationship with him!

Over thousands of years, humans came to learn a lot about the fish of the sea. We learned first from surprise sightings, then watching for signs of their presence, and then figuring out their patterns of behavior and interacting with them.

> **FACT**: The people who have made a lot of the most important first discoveries of fish are fishermen, because they are out on the water all day and night spending time with the fish. Today, fishermen continue to make startling discoveries, and often team up with scientists to help them understand the ocean better.

Our relationship with God has similar gradual stages. We start to get to know him when he surprises us by showing us he's there. Then we watch for signs of his presence. We get to know how he acts and speaks with us, and we begin to interact with him personally. The more time we spend with him—in prayer, reading the Bible, and participating in the sacraments—the more we notice him, get to know him, and love him. You're spending time with him right now by reading this devotional. As you begin this journey, think about the ways you spend time with God to get to know him better. How do you think you might go a little deeper with him on this journey?

Prayer Prompt

Lord, thank you for always being near me. I want to spend time with you to get to know you better. Help me to make special time for us every day. I know you will always meet me at these times—thanks for always showing up!

Seafarer's Challenge

Fishermen often have favorite times and places to go out and look for fish. You need those too! Choose two times (e.g., when you wake up, before meals, before bed, etc.) and places (e.g., your room, the walk to school, under your favorite tree, in church, etc.) for you to spend special time with God in prayer. And then go do it.

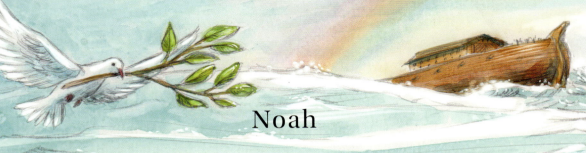

Noah

The earth was filled with violence. And God saw that the earth was corrupt; for all flesh had corrupted its ways upon the earth. And God said to Noah, "I have determined to make an end of all flesh, for the earth is filled with violence because of them; now I am going to destroy them along with the earth. Make yourself an ark of cypress wood; make rooms in the ark, and cover it inside and out with pitch. This is how you are to make it: the length of the ark three hundred cubits, its width fifty cubits, and its height thirty cubits. Make a roof for the ark, and finish it to a cubit above; and put the door of the ark in its side; make it with lower, second, and third decks. For my part, I am going to bring a flood of waters on the earth, to destroy from under heaven all flesh in which is the breath of life; everything that is on the earth shall die. But I will establish my covenant with you; and you shall come into the ark, you, your sons, your wife, and your sons' wives with you. And of every living thing, of all flesh, you shall bring two of every kind into the ark, to keep them alive with you; they shall be male and female. Of the birds according to their kinds, and of the animals according to their kinds, of every creeping thing of the ground according to its kind, two of every kind shall come in to you, to keep them alive. Also take with you every kind of food that is eaten, and store it up; and it shall serve as food for you and for them." Noah did this; he did all that God commanded him.

    The rain fell on the earth forty days and forty nights . . . the waters swelled above the mountains, covering them. . . . And all flesh died that moved on the earth . . . Only Noah was left, and those that were with him in the ark. And the waters swelled on the earth for one hundred fifty days.

But God remembered Noah and all the . . . animals that were with him in the ark. And God made a wind blow over the earth, and the waters subsided. . . . The ark came to rest on the mountains of Ararat.

Noah opened the window of the ark that he had made and sent out the dove from the ark; and the dove came back to him in the evening, and there in its beak was a freshly plucked olive leaf; so Noah knew that the waters had subsided from the earth. Then he waited another seven days, and sent out the dove; and it did not return to him any more.

Noah removed the covering of the ark, and looked, and saw that the face of the ground was drying. . . . Then God said to Noah, "Go out of the ark, you and your wife, and your sons and your sons' wives with you. Bring out with you every living thing that is with you . . . so that they may abound on the earth, and be fruitful and multiply on the earth." So Noah went out with his sons and his wife and his sons' wives.

Then God said to Noah and to his sons with him, "As for me, I am establishing my covenant with you and your descendants after you, and with every living creature that is with you, the birds, the domestic animals, and every animal of the earth with you, as many as came out of the ark. I establish my covenant with you, that never again shall all flesh be cut off by the waters of a flood, and never again shall there be a flood to destroy the earth." God said, "This is the sign of the covenant that I make between me and you and every living creature that is with you, for all future generations: I have set my bow in the clouds, and it shall be a sign of the covenant between me and the earth. . . . When the bow is in the clouds, I will see it and remember the everlasting covenant between God and every living creature of all flesh that is on the earth." God said to Noah, "This is the sign of the covenant that I have established between me and all flesh that is on the earth."

Genesis 6:11–22; 7:12, 20, 21, 23–24; 8:1, 4, 6, 10–12, 13, 15–18; 9:8–13, 16–17

DAY 3
Setting Sail

In this story it rained for forty days straight, but did you notice how many days the waters swelled over the earth? 150 days. And if we read the entire story in the Bible, it says Noah was stuck in that ark with all those animals for an entire year! Now, we can be pretty sure that the story of Noah's ark isn't an exact scientific report. We don't know exactly how big the flood was, how many animals were on the ark, or for how long. After all, the understanding of the "whole world" was much smaller then, and time wasn't kept in the same way. But like the two creation stories, the story of Noah was inspired by God so that we could learn some real truths about ourselves and him! So let's put ourselves on that ark with Noah for a whole year and see what truths the Lord might have to show us!

An ark full of animals for a whole year would be an awfully smelly place. Noah and his family would have been busy caring for the animals to make sure they survived. They had to ensure the animals were fed and watered, that they weren't injured from the tossing of the boat, and that the stalls were clean . . . which means they had to shovel a LOT of poop.

> **FACT**: During the 1500s, horses were gradually re-introduced to North America by the Spanish. The Spanish had to transport those horses across the Atlantic Ocean. The journey was extremely dangerous for the horses, and nearly half died along the

way. To keep the horses from being tossed around and injured by the pitching waves, the sailors created slings for them so that they could swing with the ship's motion. Still, being kept in the dark, unable to exercise, and near their own poop for too long made the horses sick. Only the strongest made it to shore.

If Noah's animals all survived the voyage—and it seems they all did—then he and his family must have worked really hard to keep them healthy and safe.

Sometimes God needs us to do jobs that stink. These could be dirty jobs, like cleaning out the kitchen garbage bin or changing a diaper; chores we hate, like washing dishes; or responsibilities that make us uncomfortable, like going to Confession. It's easy to shrug these things off as unimportant, thinking that God doesn't care or that these tasks don't make a difference. But they do. The smallest sacrifices we make to take care of others and ourselves are precious to God and make the world a better place.

Imagine if Noah had said "Ew, no" to shoveling horse poop off the ark. Or if he had said yes but put it off, figuring the horses would be okay for a few more days . . . they all could have gotten sick and died. But because he made that little sacrifice every day, doing a job that was awkward and gross, every animal thrived! When we commit to responsibilities that stink, we can do them out of love, knowing that God trusts us with them to make the world a better place.

 Prayer Prompt

Lord, I have some responsibilities I really hate. My least favorite is _____ _____. It's hard for me to see why it's important, and I just don't want to do it. Help me to remember how Noah shoveled all kinds of poop off that ark because he loved the animals you wanted to save, and he loved you. I may not love this responsibility, but I will do it because I love the people around me, and I love you. Help me to be generous in my love, like Noah, even when it's hard.

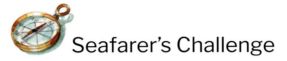 ## Seafarer's Challenge

Look around your house. What is one chore that you could do that would really help your family? Start doing it, and ask God to help you do it with love. If your chores make you want to grumble, remember Noah, and ask him to pray for you.

DAY 4
Deep Dive

Humans have been using wooden boats to brave the seas for thousands of years.

> **FACT**: The earliest recorded evidence for boats dates them back to 4000 years BC in Egypt, and they were likely around long before that. Ancient Egyptians sailed on the Nile, the Red Sea, and the Mediterranean Sea. In North America, the Haida people made dugout canoes from large red cedars that were so big and sturdy that they could be taken out on the Pacific Ocean. The Polynesian people used double-hulled vessels that could carry entire families along with their supplies and farm animals. These were likely the first people to brave the open sea to discover new lands.

People took boats onto the open seas for all kinds of reasons: to hunt for food; to escape from war, famine, or disease; to connect with people in other places to trade knowledge and goods. But in all these cases, two things were true:

The waters of the sea could save people and bring new life.

The waters of the sea could bring death.

You see, no matter how experienced or resourceful people were, water was still powerful, unpredictable, and dangerous. Even today, when our modern technology helps people to build sturdier boats, predict the weather, and keep ships afloat, there are still thousands of deaths at sea each year.

We see this in Noah's story. The waters of the massive flood were dangerous. They brought death to a world that was filled with violence, corruption, and sin. But these waters were also renewing. They stopped a cycle of violence and sin and brought the chance for a new life of goodness and joy. This is actually part of the reason that we are baptized with water.

Noah had to pass through the waters to give up his old life for a new life, dying to his old world and stepping into a new one. When we are baptized, we experience something similar! The word "baptism" actually means "plunge." When we "plunge" into the water during Baptism, we are dying to our own sin with Jesus. When we emerge from the water again, we rise up with Jesus as a "new creature." We die to our old life as our sin is washed away, and we take on a new life as a person who belongs entirely to Jesus Christ!

If you have been baptized, you have actually entered into a new life, and are part of a new family—God's family.

Prayer Prompt

Lord, thank you for the gift of a new life through Baptism! In Baptism, you wash away my sin, and you bring me into your family, where I have a place to belong forever. Help me to be faithful to my Baptism by staying true to you, and by living for you and for others.

Sailor's Log

 Draw or journal about the day you received Baptism. If you were baptized as a baby, you might have to ask your parents or another adult about it. Where were you baptized? Did they submerge your whole body in water or did they pour water over your head? How did you react? How do you think God reacted when you came through the water belonging especially to him as his child? What would you like to say to God about your Baptism?

 If you haven't been baptized yet, draw or journal about what it might mean to you to be baptized one day.

God's Promise to Abraham

The angel of the Lord called to Abraham a second time from heaven, and said, "By myself I have sworn, says the Lord: Because you have done this, and have not withheld your son, your only son, I will indeed bless you, and I will make your offspring as numerous as the stars of heaven and as the sand that is on the seashore. And your offspring shall possess the gate of their enemies, and by your offspring shall all the nations of the earth gain blessing for themselves, because you have obeyed my voice."

Genesis 22:15–18

DAY 5
Setting Sail

Abraham was a descendant of Noah. He followed, loved, and trusted God, but he was still getting to know him. Abraham and his wife, Sarah, traveled to a land that God promised to give to him and his descendants. But there was just one problem—Sarah couldn't have children.

Miraculously, when they were way too old to have children, Abraham and Sarah had a son named Isaac. Isaac could carry on Abraham's name and fulfill God's promise to give the new land to his descendants. But one day, Abraham heard God asking him to sacrifice Isaac as an offering. . . . Although it was common in those days for people to sacrifice a child to their gods, God did not really want Abraham to do this. Instead, God was going to use this general custom to bring Abraham to a deeper understanding of who God is. Abraham knew God well enough to love and trust him even with the life of his son, so he went to sacrifice Isaac. That's when God stopped him. Abraham and Isaac both proved their faithfulness to God that day, and God taught them that he wasn't like the false gods who needed child sacrifices. Because of Abraham's trust, God blessed him with the promise that his descendants would be "as numerous as the sand on the seashore."

Abraham had a lot of descendants through his twelve great-grandsons, who were the heads of the twelve tribes of Israel. But to become as numerous as the sands on the seashore, his descendants would have to be beyond counting. God really did make that happen, but in a very surprising way. . . .

Do you know how sand on the seashore is made?

> **FACT**: Most sand is created by wind and water breaking down rocks over time. But some sands are made differently. In Bermuda, pink beaches are made of sand from broken-down shells. And in Hawaii, white beaches are made of sand that comes from parrotfish poop. Parrotfish eat things off of coral reefs and swallow some of the coral. They can't digest the coral, so it gets broken down inside them and pooped out as sand!

There is so much sand on the seashore because sand comes from *many different things* breaking down—rocks, shells, organisms, and coral. And Abraham has so many descendants—beyond counting—because God brought people from *many different nations* to be part of his family.

Jesus' apostles were genetic descendants of Abraham. When Jesus sent them to baptize people from every nation, they were bringing people into the family of God, a family God built through Abraham. This means that when we are baptized, we are adopted into the family of Abraham through our faith. We become descendants of Abraham, even if we aren't genetically related to him. So across history, there really are more people who are descendants of Abraham than we can count, and there will be many more!

If you are baptized, you are part of the family of God, and you are a descendant of Abraham. What does it feel like to be part of such an ancient heritage? Have you ever thought of yourself as part of God's family before?

 ## Prayer Prompt

Lord, you have brought me into an amazing family, and an amazing heritage. Help me to love you as the father of this family, and to love all my fellow Christians as brothers and sisters. And, when the time is right, inspire me to invite others to join your family too!

 ## Seafarer's Challenge

Look up the date of your Baptism. That day is like your "birthday" into the family of God! Mark that day down on your calendar and start doing something to celebrate it every year. Or if you haven't been baptized yet, take a moment to talk to God about it. Do you feel him inviting you to join his family?

DAY 6

Deep Dive

Abraham was born in Ur of the Chaldeans, in modern day Iraq. From his hometown, he couldn't see a seashore. But if he ever traveled east, or knew anyone who had, he would have known about the beaches on the Persian Gulf.

> **FACT**: One of the most famous beaches of the Persian Gulf is on the island of Hormuz. Because of the high amounts of iron oxide in the soil, a lot of the ground in Hormuz has a red tinge to it. In places like the Red Beach, the sand is a very noticeable red color. When sea waves lap against the seashore, they naturally stir up sand. On the Red Beach, the waves that come up to shore turn pink or red.

Today, we know that in different parts of the world seashore sand can be brown, tan, cream, golden, red, pink, orange, purple, green, white, or black. Abraham might not have known all of this, but he would have known quite a bit from his travels and from hearing stories.

When the Lord promised to make Abraham's descendants "as numerous as the sand on the seashore," Abraham was given a hint as to what his family would look like. It meant that they would be too many to count, of course. But it also suggested that they would be diverse, just like the sands on seashores.

Sands are different colors based on where they come from. Black sand comes from volcanic rocks, whereas white sand might come from quartz . . . or parrotfish poop. These differences make seashores fascinating! We people are like that too.

The Catholic Church is universal, which means that our faith is shared by people all over the world from different cultures and backgrounds. This makes our faith family beautiful and interesting. All Catholics have the same faith, the same Creed, and the same Pope. But did you know that there are different Catholic rites? You can go to a Catholic Mass in any of the Catholic rites and you will be at a real Mass, where you can receive the Eucharist and be united in faith, but there might some differences in the traditions, languages, or actions. Do you know what Catholic rite you attend Mass in? In North America, the Roman (or Latin) rite is the most common, but Catholics might also celebrate Mass in the Maronite rite, Byzantine rite, Malabar rite, or Chaldean rite, just to name a few. (Can you guess where most Chaldean Catholics are originally from? Hint: Abraham was originally from the same area!)

Whichever rite you celebrate in the Catholic Church, your background and traditions bring beauty to the life of all Catholics! What is one tradition that you love about your rite? How do you think it can help people have a feeling of belonging or some other experience of God? Have you ever heard of things that Catholics do in other rites? What is one tradition from another Catholic rite that you think is cool? How does it deepen your understanding of who we are as Catholics?

Prayer Prompt

Lord, you love to see all your unique children united together in their love for you. Thank you for making me part of this diverse but united family in the Catholic Church. Help me to appreciate my traditions and to celebrate the traditions of other Catholics too. Help us feel united as one.

 Seafarer's Challenge

Look up a Catholic saint who grew up in a different Catholic rite than you. Do you go to a Roman Catholic church? Then try looking up a Maronite Catholic saint, like Saint Charbel. Do you go to a Byzantine Catholic church? Then try looking up a Malabar Catholic saint, like Saint Kuriakose Elias Chavara. Find a saint from another rite who really inspires you, and write your own prayer to ask him or her to pray for you in your life.

Moses Parts the Red Sea

When the king of Egypt was told that the people had fled, the minds of Pharaoh and his officials were changed toward the people, and they said, "What have we done, letting Israel leave our service?" So he had his chariot made ready, and took his army with him; he took six hundred picked chariots and all the other chariots of Egypt with officers over all of them. The Lord hardened the heart of Pharaoh king of Egypt and he pursued the Israelites, who were going out boldly. The Egyptians pursued them, all Pharaoh's horses and chariots, his chariot drivers and his army; they overtook them camped by the sea. . . .

As Pharaoh drew near, the Israelites looked back, and there were the Egyptians advancing on them. In great fear the Israelites cried out to the Lord . . . . But Moses said to the people, "Do not be afraid, stand firm, and see the deliverance that the Lord will accomplish for you today; for the Egyptians whom you see today you shall never see again. The Lord will fight for you, and you have only to keep still."

Then the Lord said to Moses, "Why do you cry out to me? Tell the Israelites to go forward. But you lift up your staff, and stretch out your hand over the sea and divide it, that the Israelites may go into the sea on dry ground. . . ."

The angel of God who was going before the Israelite army moved and went behind them; and the pillar of cloud moved from in front of them and took its place behind them. It came between the army of Egypt and the army of Israel. And so the cloud was there with the darkness, and it lit up the night; one did not come near the other all night.

Then Moses stretched out his hand over the sea. The Lord drove the sea back by a strong east wind all night, and turned the sea into dry land; and the waters were divided. The Israelites went into the sea on dry ground, the waters forming a wall for them on their right and on their left. The Egyptians pursued, and went into the sea after them, all of Pharaoh's horses, chariots, and chariot drivers. At the morning watch the Lord in the pillar of fire and cloud looked down upon the Egyptian army, and threw the Egyptian army into panic. He clogged their chariot wheels so that they turned with difficulty. The Egyptians said, "Let us flee from the Israelites, for the Lord is fighting for them. . . ."

Then the Lord said to Moses, "Stretch out your hand over the sea, so that the water may come back upon the Egyptians, upon their chariots and chariot drivers." So Moses stretched out his hand over the sea, and at dawn the sea returned to its normal depth. As the Egyptians fled before it, the Lord tossed the Egyptians into the sea. The waters returned and covered the chariots and the chariot drivers, the entire army of Pharaoh that had followed them into the sea; not one of them remained. But the Israelites walked on dry ground through the sea, the waters forming a wall for them on their right and on their left.

Thus the Lord saved Israel that day from the Egyptians.

Exodus 14: 5–9, 10, 13–16, 19–25, 26–30

DAY 7
Setting Sail

The Israelites were the Jewish descendants of Abraham through his son Isaac. They were enslaved in Egypt for many years. Finally, after generations of waiting, the Lord raised up Moses to lead his people out of Egypt by crossing the Red Sea. In art and movies, when Moses parts the Red Sea it looks like the water divides immediately. But look back at the story. Is that what actually happened?

God used an east wind to divide the water, and it took all night. It was a miracle, but he let it take time. Can you imagine what it was like for the Israelites to wait with the Egyptian soldiers just on the other side of the cloud? Probably no one slept very well. But Moses told them that the Lord was fighting for them, and that they just had to be still and let God be God.

FACT: When sailors want to dock their boat or sail out of port, they have to time everything according to the tides. At high tide, there is a lot of motion in the water, and at low tide it is easy for a boat to run aground. But there is a short window of time called "slack tide," when the water is not moving in or out. Slack tide is the safest time for boats to navigate, and it's ideal for scuba divers too! Slack tide doesn't last long, so sailors and divers need to be patient and wait for the right time to come, and then go immediately once it does!

That is what the Israelites had to do beside the Red Sea—wait patiently for God to work in his own timing and be ready to go when the way was cleared.

Waiting for God can be hard. We want things done right away. It can be frustrating when God seems to have a different idea. But we also know that if God is taking time to do something in our lives, it is because he knows something we don't know. His timing is always perfect. So we have to be still, and let God be God.

Being still doesn't mean just sitting around. What did Moses do while he waited for God? He watched. He listened. He prayed. He took care of the Israelites. Because he was watching, listening, and praying, he heard God tell him what to do to save everyone. Because he worked hard to help his people, he knew what they needed. When Moses was being still, he was keeping himself open to God. God was doing a lot in the hearts of all the Israelites before they were ready to walk across the sea to freedom.

Is there something in your life that you asked God to help you with, but are still waiting for? Waiting might be a time for you to be still and listen. What might God be trying to work in your heart before you are ready for this thing you are hoping for? Is God helping prepare other people for it too? Take some time to ask him about it today. Then wait, watch, listen, pray, and serve, like Moses. Be still, because the Lord is fighting for you.

 **Prayer Prompt**

Lord, thank you for always being with me, for loving me, and for fighting for me. I believe that you really know what's best for me, and will do it when everything is ready. I am really hoping for _____
_____ in my life. If it is your will, help me to be still while I am waiting for you to work it in my life. If it is not your will, help me to be still and listen for the even bigger dream you have for me.

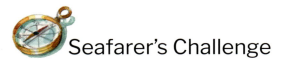 ## Seafarer's Challenge

Take some time to just sit quietly with God today. Choose a quiet place, sit down, and remember he is with you. Maybe you will hear him speak in your heart or maybe he will sit with you quietly, but just sitting together is the point. When we really love someone, it is being with them that is the most important thing, even when we are both quiet.

DAY 8

Deep Dive

"The Lord hardened the heart of Pharaoh. . . ." This phrase kind of sounds like God made Pharoah not listen to him on purpose, but that's actually not what it means. In Scripture, when God says that he will harden the heart of someone, he isn't saying he is going to make that person unable to listen to him. He is saying that is the reaction the person is going to have to his words. In fact, before this story in Exodus 8, it explicitly says that Pharaoh hardened his own heart, showing us that Pharaoh was choosing not to listen to God's words. And God, respecting Pharaoh's free will, let him choose this.

> **FACT**: In the Red Sea, there is a species of fish called the porcupine fish, which lives in the coral reefs. It has strong little spines all over it, making it look a bit like a porcupine. When a porcupine fish feels threatened, it quickly swallows so much water that it puffs up enormously, making its sharp spines stick out so that nothing can touch or swallow it.

In a way, people do this too. When we feel threatened, we often get defensive and stop listening. We puff up our pride and harden our hearts and start to argue about why we are right and they are wrong, without actually hearing what they have to say. We don't listen so that we don't have to be wrong, and we don't have to change.

When the Lord says in Scripture that he is going to harden someone's heart, he means that, sadly, he knows that this person is going to get defensive and refuse to listen. When he tries to speak to them, that is the reaction they are going to have. They will be too busy trying to be right to listen to the voice of the one who is trying to help them.

We often act like a porcupine fish and puff ourselves up when people try to confront us about a problem, even when they are really just trying to help us. And, like Pharaoh and his soldiers, we can harden our hearts when God tries to guide us in a better direction because we don't want to admit we are wrong or that we need to change something. But that means that we push away God's love and reject the life he is trying to give us.

We don't want hard hearts—we want open ones.

Have you ever heard of an "examen" prayer? It's a traditional practice that people do every day to help them keep their hearts open to the Lord. At the end of the day, we take a few minutes to look back and think about everything that happened that day and how we reacted. We notice what happened, how we felt, what we thought, and what we did. And we ask ourselves:

Where was God reaching out to me today? I thank God for his presence.

When did I accept God's gifts today? I thank God for everything I have received!

When did I not notice God acting? I ask God to help me recognize him there next time.

When did I not accept God's gifts, or not share them with others? I ask God's forgiveness and ask him to help me to be more open tomorrow.

This way we go to bed with a grateful and open heart and are closer to God instead of further away.

Prayer Prompt

Lord, I don't want my heart to harden when you speak to me—I want to be open to listen, so that I can grow closer to you. Help me to be open to listening to you, even when you are helping me to change something in my life. I know you do this because you love me.

Sailor's Log

Pray the examen today, using the questions above. What were some of the best things you noticed God doing? What is one thing you want to do better tomorrow? Write it all here.

Leviathan

O Lord, how manifold are your works!
    In wisdom you have made them all;
    the earth is full of your creatures.
Yonder is the sea, great and wide,
    creeping things innumerable are there,
    living things both small and great.
There go the ships,
    and Leviathan that you formed to sport in it.

. . . I will sing to the Lord as long as I live;
    I will sing praise to my God while I have being.
May my meditation be pleasing to him,
    for I rejoice in the Lord.

Psalm 104:24–26, 33–34

DAY 9
Setting Sail

Did you catch that? God made the Leviathan (leh VIE uh thin) "to sport," or to play, in the sea. God made the Leviathan *playful*.

When people hear "Leviathan" they usually think about how dangerous it sounds. They aren't wrong. From the Bible's description in Job 41, the Leviathan is terrifying.

> **FACT**: The Leviathan is a sea monster in ancient Jewish legend that was so dangerous that no man could kill it. While we don't know what real animal might have inspired these legends, one fairly recent discovery got scientists thinking! In 2008, scientists discovered the fossilized skull and jaw of a 43-foot-long whale with 14-inch teeth—a super-predator related to modern sperm whales. Although it didn't exactly fit the description in Job, its size, teeth, and strength were similar enough for the scientists to name it *Livyatan melvillei*.

The Leviathan was portrayed as a super predator, too. But the Bible also tells us there is more to the Leviathan than just being scary.

God gave each creature, even dangerous ones, good and special qualities that reveal some of God's own characteristics. For example, graceful blue sharks can teach us that God is beautiful. Community-oriented orcas can teach us that God brings us together. The Leviathan can teach us that God has a playful side too!

It's easy to think of Jesus being serious, teaching, or healing. And he did all those things. But he also smiled, got excited, cheered, and laughed. Have you ever thought of how Jesus liked to play when he was a kid? Or what he did for fun with the apostles?

God likes to have fun. God the Son, Jesus, rejoiced with the disciples in the New Testament. God the Father rejoiced over the playfulness of the Leviathan. God rejoices in your excitement too! Maybe you go to God when you are sad, or when you need something. But do you share your fun with him too? You can do it by simply flashing a grin up at the sky that's meant just for him or thanking him for being with you as you enjoy something. As you experience how God rejoices over you, you will in turn begin to rejoice over who God is, and what he is doing in you.

Prayer Prompt

Lord, sometimes I forget that you don't want to be only my teacher and my guide—you also want to be my friend. Help me to learn how to have fun with you. Help me to learn to recognize when you're actually smiling at me, and that I can actually smile back. Here's to lots of new adventures together!

Glory to the Father, and to the Son, and to the Holy Spirit! As it was in the beginning, is now, and ever shall be, world without end. Amen.

Sailor's Log

Look up the description of the Leviathan: It's in the Bible, the book of Job, chapter 41. Try to imagine this creature having fun in the water (lots of sea creatures jump, spin, or make noises for fun!). See if you can draw it playing in a way that makes you smile the way God smiles.

DAY 10

Deep Dive

Did you read the description in Job 41? The Leviathan does NOT sound like an appealing-looking animal. Cool? Yes. Nice-looking? No. But in this psalm, the writer praises God for it. It makes sense to look at a beautiful animal and praise God: Siberian tigers, eastern coral snakes, and box jellyfish are all beautiful. But the Leviathan?

When a creature looks strange to us, we don't usually look harder to see the beauty God placed in it.

> **FACT**: Take the vampire squid. This deep-water creature gets its name from its red eyes and the cape-like skin that connects its eight arms. It might not look too garish when it's calm, but a frightened vampire squid will reverse the cape-like part of its body to cover its head, revealing creepy long spines on the back of its arms. This squid looks creepy, but it's not venomous, and it doesn't suck blood. It's safe!

But most people take one look, make a face, and run. It's hard to think twice about a strange-looking animal.

But the writer of this psalm did think twice about the Leviathan—he took the time to consider it again. And that was how he noticed that God made the Leviathan so playful.

When we meet someone different, we often don't look harder to find the gift of God in them. Maybe we don't like someone's manners or the way they look. Maybe we can't understand them when they talk. Maybe they're hard to figure out. So we turn and look away. But if we do this, we will never know if they are playful, loyal, generous, smart, funny, thoughtful, helpful, or kind. We look away before we realize how amazing God made them. We miss learning more about them, and we miss learning more about God.

Think of one, two, or three people in your life that you really don't find appealing. Be honest. We all have people we feel like that about. Ask God to help you take a second look at these people with new eyes, the way the psalmist looked deeper at the Leviathan. Maybe, after a few moments, a few days, or even a few years, you will discover something amazing about one of those people that will have you rejoicing and praising God for the gift that they are.

Prayer Prompt

Lord, I have to be honest. I don't find _____ very appealing. And I can't really see how you made them a gift. Help me to take a deeper look at them today, even if I don't totally want to. I want to be open to seeing the gift you made them to be.

Seafarer's Challenge

Think of one kind thing you can do for or say to one person you don't like. Come up with a strategy of how and when you will do it. Remember—you're doing this to help you recognize and honor the gift that God made them. After you do/say something kind to that person, write down here how it went.

Jonah

Now the word of the Lord came to Jonah son of Amittai, saying, "Go at once to Nineveh, that great city, and cry out against it; for their wickedness has come up before me." But Jonah set out to flee to Tarshish from the presence of the Lord. He . . . found a ship going to Tarshish . . . paid his fare and went on board, to go . . . away from the presence of the Lord.

But the Lord hurled a great wind upon the sea, and such a mighty storm came upon the sea that the ship threatened to break up. Then the mariners were afraid, and each cried to his god. They threw the cargo that was in the ship into the sea, to lighten it for them. Jonah, meanwhile, had gone down into the hold of the ship and had lain down, and was fast asleep. The captain came and said to him, "What are you doing sound asleep? Get up, call on your god! Perhaps the god will spare us a thought so that we do not perish."

The sailors . . . said to him, "Tell us why this calamity has come upon us. What is your occupation? Where do you come from? What is your country? And of what people are you?" "I am a Hebrew," he replied. "I worship the Lord, the God of heaven, who made the sea and the dry land." Then the men were even more afraid, and said to him, "What is this that you have done!" For the men knew that he was fleeing from the presence of the Lord, because he had told them so.

Then they said to him, "What shall we do to you, that the sea may quiet down for us?" For the sea was growing more and more tempestuous. He said to them, "Pick me up and throw me into the sea; then the sea will quiet down for you; for I know it is because of me that this great storm has come upon you." Nevertheless the men rowed hard to bring the ship back to land, but they could not, for the sea grew more and more stormy against them. Then they cried out to the Lord, "Please, O Lord, we pray, do not let us perish on account of this man's life. Do not make us guilty of innocent blood; for you, O Lord, have done as it pleased you." So they picked Jonah up and threw him into the sea; and the sea ceased from its raging. Then the men feared the Lord even more, and they offered a sacrifice to the Lord and made vows.

But the Lord provided a large fish to swallow up Jonah; and Jonah was in the belly of the fish three days and three nights.

Then Jonah prayed to the Lord his God from the belly of the fish, saying,

"I called to the Lord out of my distress,
    and he answered me;
. . . I cried,
    and you heard my voice.
You cast me into the deep,
    into the heart of the seas,
    and the flood surrounded me;
all your waves and your billows
    passed over me. . . .
The waters closed in over me;
    the deep surrounded me;
weeds were wrapped around my head. . . .
yet you brought up my life from the Pit,
    O Lord my God.
As my life was ebbing away,
    I remembered the Lord;
and my prayer came to you . . .
    Deliverance belongs to the Lord!"

Then the Lord spoke to the fish, and it spewed Jonah out upon the dry land.

Jonah 1:1–7, 8–17; 2:1–3, 5, 6–7, 9–10

DAY 11
Setting Sail

When God asks Jonah to go to a foreign city to tell them to repent, Jonah isn't exactly thrilled. He actually refuses and literally runs in the opposite direction. And God lets him run—for a while.

> **FACT**: The Mediterranean Sea was the biggest sea that you could sail on from Israel. Its size is just under 970,000 square miles, and it touches three different continents: Europe to the north, Asia to the east, and Africa to the south.

If Jonah wanted to get away fast, it was the perfect sea to choose.

God saves Jonah from drowning by sending a fish to gulp him up whole. Even though Jonah was running away, God still saved him. And when Jonah was finally spewed out onto dry land, God asked him again to go tell the foreign city to repent. But notice that after the fish spit Jonah out, God didn't make a bird snatch him and bring him to that city. He didn't force Jonah to agree. He simply asked him again. And he trusted Jonah to listen.

God does this with us, too. He asks us things. But he doesn't force us to do them. He trusts us to listen to him out of love. He gives us the free will to decide to follow him, and to choose to do the right thing. That means that every time we accept God's love, we are choosing to love him. Every time we show love to another person, we are choosing to share the love God gives us.

When Jonah jumped onto that boat, it could have taken him anywhere along the coast of Europe, Asia, or Africa. But in the end, he did choose to go where the Lord was sending him. When we have to make a decision, there are always lots of things we could do instead, but we have the freedom to choose what the Lord is asking us to choose. If we mess up and choose the wrong thing, he doesn't abandon us, just like he didn't abandon Jonah. We might still have to face the consequences of our bad decision, like Jonah did, but God will pull us through. In his love and mercy, he gives us another chance to choose him.

Prayer Prompt

Lord, thank you for never leaving me. I am sorry for all the times I mess up or choose something that doesn't bring me closer to you. Help me to use the freedom you gave me to choose the good, and to always choose you.

Seafarer's Challenge

What is one area in your life where you could choose God more often? It could be a situation with your friends or strangers, with your family or by yourself. Write down what you can do to choose God in this situation. How can you bring him into your next decision?

DAY 12
Deep Dive

It can be overwhelming to go through hard situations when we don't know why we have to be there. Maybe you go to a school where classmates pick on you. Or you come home to your family fighting. Or you hate practicing an instrument but have to take lessons. Or you want to comfort a sick loved one but don't know what to do or say. In situations like this, we might wonder why God doesn't take us out of them, or what he expects us to do. God might actually show us through the story of Jonah. Except he doesn't show us with Jonah—he shows us with the fish.

Think of this from the fish's perspective. The fish was in the middle of a storm, struggling to swim straight, and quite hungry. When it thought it had found a snack, it just got a pain-in-the-stomach—Jonah. This poor fish wasn't the only sea creature to swallow the wrong thing.

> **FACT**: Centuries ago, scientists cut open a shark to examine the contents of its stomach. They were astounded by what was inside . . . a full suit of armour. A French physician named Guillaume Rondelet wrote about the incident in the 1500s. No one quite knows exactly how the shark found a whole suit of armour—did a knight fall off a boat in a storm? did a merchant lose it at sea?—but the poor shark thought it was getting a full meal out of what would become a pain in its stomach.

Our poor fish threw Jonah up after a few days. It had zero clue about what was going on. It was just doing what fish do. But because it was doing what fish are supposed to do, because it showed up where it needed to be, God used it to save Jonah's life!

This is the key for us. We don't always understand what is going on, and we can't always see what God is doing in our lives. But when we show up, when we do what we are supposed to do, then God can bring love, courage, comfort, kindness, and goodness into the world through us. In this case, he worked through the fish to save Jonah from drowning and then to save an entire city with Jonah's preaching. If God can use a fish, who showed up to do fish things, to save an entire city, then imagine what he can do with you! When things get rough, we can trust that if we keep following God's commands to love him and love our neighbor we will be instruments of grace, change, and forgiveness, even when we don't realize it.

Prayer Prompt

Lord, honestly, I just don't get why I have to _____ _____. Help me to figure out what it means to love you and love others in situations like this, so that I can at least help bring you to the people around me, even if I can't see right away how it will work out.

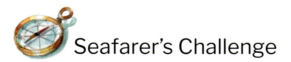
Seafarer's Challenge

What is one responsibility you have that you just don't understand why, or how, you are supposed to do it? Make or get a fish token/symbol that you can carry around. Next time you need to tackle this responsibility, put the fish in your pocket to remind you that God wants to use your presence to bring something good to this situation. Try to notice what that good might be.

Daniel

". . . Bless the Lord, seas and rivers;
  sing praise to him and highly exalt him forever.
Bless the Lord, you whales and all that swim in the waters;
  sing praise to him and highly exalt him forever.
Bless the Lord, all birds of the air;
  sing praise to him and highly exalt him forever.
Bless the Lord, all wild animals and cattle;
  sing praise to him and highly exalt him forever.

"Bless the Lord, all people on earth;
    sing praise to him and highly exalt him forever.
Bless the Lord, O Israel;
    sing praise to him and highly exalt him forever.
Bless the Lord, you priests of the Lord;
    sing praise to him and highly exalt him forever.
Bless the Lord, you servants of the Lord;
    sing praise to him and highly exalt him forever.
Bless the Lord, spirits and souls of the righteous;
    sing praise to him and highly exalt him forever.
Bless the Lord, you who are holy and humble in heart;
    sing praise to him and highly exalt him forever."

Daniel 3:78–87

DAY 13
Setting Sail

This prayer was shouted out loudly by three faithful young Jewish men. Their names were Azariah, Hananiah, and Mishael. They were not at a celebration in the Jewish temple or at a religious festival with their families. They were in the middle of a fire that a foreign king had thrown them into to try to kill them for worshipping the one God. But God protected them from the flames. They freaked out a lot of people by walking around in the middle of the fire, singing and praying. Their Jewish friend Daniel saw it all happen and wrote it down.

Daniel, Hananiah, Azariah, and Mishael were in Babylon, a country where people hated them for worshipping the Lord, instead of worshipping the Babylonian gods. The young men had been exiled from their home in Israel. Really, it seemed like they didn't belong in Babylon at all. But God used them to touch the hearts of a kingdom.

In their prayer, they list creatures that live in harmony with the sea: whales, fish, birds, and people. But next in the list is "wild animals and cattle." That kind of sticks out, because it seems like they are moving their list away from the sea. But actually, there are wild animals that live in harmony with the sea too.

FACT: Sea wolves are wolves that evolved differently from regular wolves to thrive on the ocean coast. Found mostly in the Vancouver Island area, their genetic differences make them incredible swimmers—they can swim almost eight miles between islands in the Pacific Ocean! They are much smaller than regular wolves, and the bulk of their diet is based on seafood.

If you saw a wolf swimming in the Pacific Ocean you might assume it didn't belong there and that it was going to drown. But God made sure these wolves would have just what they need to survive in ocean environments and to help balance their habitats too.

Sometimes we have to go places where we don't fit in. But God doesn't let us go to these places alone. In our Baptism and in Confirmation, we are given the grace to bring God wherever we go and to build up his kingdom. God will give us the courage, strength, and abilities we need to survive really strange situations. And just like Azariah and his companions, when we act faithfully and honestly we can inspire people who didn't even like us at first. We can inspire them to want to get to know our God when they see that we bring peace and joy with us wherever we go.

So don't be afraid to go into places where you don't fit in. Tackle the situation the way the sea wolf tackles the ocean. And bring God with you as Azariah, Hananiah, and Mishael did. You might help to bring God to someone who needs him.

Prayer Prompt

Lord, I hate feeling like I don't fit in. But I know that if I have to go to a place where I don't fit in, you will want me there for some reason. Help me to bring your grace and peace wherever I go.

Sailor's Log

Write your own prayer of praise, like the one these three young men prayed. What elements of nature, animals, or people would you tell to praise the Lord? Try to come up with at least seven.

DAY 14

Deep Dive

In this section of the prayer of the young men, they are telling the waters and the creatures in them to sing praise to God. This might seem a bit odd at first: What are they saying? That the sea can sing? That fish can form their own little choir? That they can praise the Lord?

Actually, that is exactly what they're saying. And they aren't wrong.

There is a lot of sound going on underwater, and it really can sound magical!

FACT: People who grow up by large lakes—some of which have traditionally been called "seas"—that freeze over in the winter have heard the many "voices" of water. They hear the lapping and splashing that we are all used to hearing, but they also know the sound of frozen water. If you walk out onto a safely frozen lake and put your ear to the ice, you will discover that ice has sounds. These sounds, which you can sometimes hear even from a distance, are caused by the shifting of the ice. Many people describe this as the ice singing. And underwater, scientists have been slowly discovering new sounds that fish make. Different fish make different noises, like croaking, buzzing, squawking, popping, chirping, or humming. Oyster toadfish may look kind of ugly, but they can contract certain muscles to make a really cool

sound similar to a fog horn or boat whistle. Scientists even recently discovered that there are some fish that sing at dawn and at dusk, just as some birds do!

It is fascinating that fish and birds sing at dawn and dusk, because these are also traditional times for people to sing prayers. Even today, Catholics continue the tradition of singing or reciting psalms in the morning and evening to begin and end each day praising the Lord. Just as birds and fish give glory to God simply by their existence, and with the beauty of their voices, we also use the beauty of our voices and our prayers to praise God each day.

Some of us have a gift for singing, and some of us . . . don't. But God always loves to hear our voices raised in song, even if no one else does. He counts every note as precious, and he rejoices at the sound of your voice. Even if you don't feel comfortable singing, try following the example of the birds, the fish, and generations of believers in beginning and ending each day by thanking God. It doesn't have to be a big wordy prayer. It can be simple and from the heart. When you wake up, thank the Lord for your life. And before you go to sleep, thank the Lord for walking with you through the day. You will start to find that the more you express gratitude, the more open you will be to hearing God's voice in your life.

Prayer Prompt

In your own words, praise the Lord for something beautiful he has said, made, or done.

Seafarer's Challenge

See how many days this week you can remember to thank God at the beginning and end of each day. Keep track of what time works best for you to remember. Before you get out of bed? While you're brushing your teeth? Before breakfast or dinner? While you are falling asleep? Pick the morning and evening times that work best, and start to make a habit of thanking God every day.

Part Two
NEW TESTAMENT

"*Duc in altum*—Put out into the deep" (Luke 5:4).

—Saint John Paul II, Angelus, February 4, 2001

Finally, it's time for the Messiah to come. Jesus is born and grows up in a little village. Most people don't know he is the Messiah. When he is thirty years old, he is ready to begin his ministry of healing, teaching, and redeeming people from their sins.

Miraculous Catch

Once while Jesus was standing beside the lake of Gennesaret, and the crowd was pressing in on him to hear the word of God, he saw two boats there at the shore of the lake; the fishermen had gone out of them and were washing their nets. He got into one of the boats, the one belonging to Simon, and asked him to put out a little way from the shore. Then he sat down and taught the crowds from the boat. When he had finished speaking, he said to Simon, "Put out into the deep water and let down your nets for a catch." Simon answered, "Master, we have worked all night long but have caught nothing. Yet if you say so, I will let down the nets." When they had done this, they caught so many fish that their nets were beginning to break. So they signaled their partners in the other boat to come and help them. And they came and filled both boats, so that they began to sink. But when Simon Peter saw it, he fell down at Jesus' knees, saying, "Go away from me, Lord, for I am a sinful man!" For he and all who were with him were amazed at the catch of fish that they had taken; and so also were James and John, sons of Zebedee, who were partners with Simon. Then Jesus said to Simon, "Do not be afraid; from now on you will be catching people." When they had brought their boats to shore, they left everything and followed him.

Luke 5:1–11

DAY 15
Setting Sail

Lake Gennesaret is another name for the Sea of Galilee (also called the Sea of Tiberias). The Sea of Galilee is a really beautiful place. It has supported fishermen for centuries. Jesus loved the Sea of Galilee; in the Gospels, we see him go there often. This is one of the first times we see Jesus teaching, when people were hungry for what he had to say but didn't yet know who he was. And here, two fishermen who were just doing their job get pulled into Jesus' life.

Simon and Andrew did have *some* idea who Jesus was. We know from the Gospel of John that Andrew had listened to Jesus' cousin, John the Baptist, telling people that Jesus was the Lamb of God. But neither of them knew what that meant. Still, when Jesus asked Simon to do something inconvenient—put his boat out on the water when Simon was trying to get his nets clean on land—Simon agreed. He let Jesus climb into his boat and interrupt his work.

FACT: Sometimes sailors are interrupted by unexpected things. A few years ago, videos were shared online of a man on his boat off the coast of British Columbia. He and his companions spotted a sea otter being chased by an orca. The sea otter saw their boat and raced toward it, jumping into it over the side at the very moment the orca was about to bite him! The sea otter was sitting near the engine, so the

> sailors could not start the engine to continue their trip as they had planned. But they decided to let the sea otter interrupt their plans and ended up saving its life.

When Simon let Jesus into his boat, he had no idea that Jesus was about to change his entire life. He definitely had no idea that he was about to leave his job, get a new name (Peter), and travel all over to help other people meet the Lord. But just like the sailors in British Columbia, Simon let himself be interrupted and that ended up changing the lives of thousands of people throughout all of history.

Sometimes Jesus asks us to do things differently. He interrupts us. It can be easy to get annoyed and not listen or to say "maybe later." But if we are open like Simon and let Jesus interrupt us, he can work through us to change people's lives.

What kind of things might Jesus ask of you that interrupt your life? Maybe it's going to church on Sundays when you would rather sleep in. Maybe it's taking time to pray before bed when you want to have another ten minutes playing your video game or reading your book. Maybe he is inspiring you to start talking to someone unpopular at school, or to ask about raising money for a charity. These things do interrupt us. But if we listen, if we say yes, and if we invite Jesus into our boat, it can change our lives and the lives of others!

Prayer Prompt

Lord, sometimes I get really comfortable in my own ways. But I know that I can't get to know you better or help other people if I don't let you interrupt me. Help me to be brave enough to take risks in letting you interrupt me! I want to be open to your surprises like Peter on the Sea of Galilee.

# Sailor's Log

Write down one way that Jesus has already tried to interrupt you. As soon as you can, let Jesus interrupt you in this way. Then record how you felt.

DAY 16

Deep Dive

Did you notice Simon's response when Jesus tells him to put his fishing nets in the water for a catch? Simon tells Jesus that he had been fishing all night and has caught absolutely nothing.

> **FACT**: Fishermen on the Sea of Galilee fished at night. In the dark, they lit torches and held them over the water. The light from the torches would attract curious fish to the side of the boat, where the fishermen could scoop them up with their nets.

Simon and Andrew—and their partners James and John—were professional fishermen. They knew what they were doing. But that night, nothing they did worked. Maybe someone made a mistake, like making a loud noise that scared the fish away. Or maybe they did everything right, but the fish never came. Either way, they failed. They didn't catch any fish, so they would have no fish to sell that day, and that meant they might not be able to buy much food. After a long and hard night, Simon admitted to Jesus that he had failed.

Maybe you already know what it's like to fail. Or maybe you haven't experienced it yet. We all fail at something eventually. But Jesus doesn't need us to be successful, and he doesn't need us to be perfect. He needs us to be open to him, and to rely on him. He needs us to be honest with him and admit our failures so that he can turn them into something else.

When we admit to Jesus that we messed up, he can help us to make things right. He is like the torch in the night, a light in the dark. He brings grace and strength and joy no matter how badly we've messed up. He can turn our failures into new opportunities. He can show us all the good things he has in store for us, because of his love for us.

Simon found that out when Jesus brought him so many fish that his boat started to sink. Jesus does that with us. He gives us so much grace we don't even know what to do with it all. But his grace helps us to see everything in a new way. It makes us brave enough to face scary things. It inspires us to bring God to other people. It frees us to love deeper. If we never fail, we might never learn some of the things Jesus wants us to know, or we might miss opportunities to meet Jesus in a life changing way.

So don't be ashamed or afraid of failure. Give your failures to Jesus, the way Simon did. Jesus will meet you in your failures, and he will change everything.

Prayer Prompt

Lord, it makes me feel a little better to know that even Peter, Andrew, James, and John failed at important stuff. I failed and messed up when _____ _____. Please come into this situation and bring something good out of it, as you did for Peter. I trust you.

Seafarer's Challenge

The next time you see someone around you fail at something, go out of your way to encourage or comfort them.

Calling Fishermen

As [Jesus] walked by the Sea of Galilee, he saw two brothers, Simon, who is called Peter, and Andrew his brother, casting a net into the sea—for they were fishermen. And he said to them, "Follow me, and I will make you fish for people." Immediately they left their nets and followed him. As he went from there, he saw two other brothers, James son of Zebedee and his brother John, in the boat with their father Zebedee, mending their nets, and he called them. Immediately they left the boat and their father, and followed him.

Matthew 4:18–22

DAY 17
Setting Sail

Does this story sound familiar? Actually, it's talking about the same event as our last Bible story. But it's told differently. Why?

This passage about Jesus calling the fishermen is written by Matthew. The last passage was written by Luke. They focus on different things that happened during the same event. In the Bible, Matthew and Luke both write about many things they witnessed themselves, but they weren't there for everything. In this case, neither of them was there to see Jesus call the four young fishermen. Both are sharing a story that was told to them by people who were actually there, and who probably remembered different things about it. This is actually really good, because it helps us see different parts of the same story and understand it more fully.

The Bible is unique. It is made up of books, poems, speeches, and letters, all written by different people. But even though a lot of people wrote different parts of the Bible, there is only one main author: God. God inspired each and every writer in the Bible to share specific stories, memories, prayers, and ideas. He guided them in their writing, so they could reveal his truths to everyone who would read what they wrote.

FACT: In the dark, flashlight fish look like they have glow-in-the-dark eyes. But the light is not coming from their eyes at all. Flashlight fish actually have a special organ under each eye that has bioluminescent bacteria inside. It's the bacteria that light up in the dark! The fish can "turn off" the light by lowering a dark lid over it (or some species rotate the organ into a pocket). The light produced by the bacteria is essential for flashlight fish. It enables the fish to find food, find a mate, and confuse predators.

If God provided these little fish with bacteria to give them light in the deep waters of the ocean, then we should not be surprised that God provided the light of understanding to the authors of Sacred Scripture. He ensured that they wrote all and only the truth his beloved children need to be saved. We can trust his promise to guide the Church in recognizing, teaching, and protecting this saving truth in Scripture, including when he inspired the Church to compile (collect) the writings of the Bible in the year 382. The light of the Holy Spirit guided the writers of the Bible and the members of the Church who compiled the Bible in their desire to communicate God's saving Truth in the way he desired to share it.

The Bible has different kinds of writings in it. Some parts are history or recorded memories. Some parts are a sharing of God's promises. Some parts are an expression of someone's personal struggle, experience, or feelings. Some parts are poems or songs. Some parts are parables, which are stories that didn't literally happen but are meant to explain something true. With all these different types of writings written by different people, at different times, and in a culture that was different from our own, we often have to stop and think about what is being communicated. Some parts are easy to understand, even thousands of years after they were written. Some parts are really hard to understand, because we don't live in the same culture or situation as the authors. But taken in the context of the whole, all of the writing is true because it was inspired by God, and God is Truth itself.

Which do you like better: the way Matthew tells this story or the way Luke tells it? Which story gives you a better understanding of what happened? Does your less favorite one help you notice different details than your favorite one?

Prayer Prompt

Lord, it's cool to see that different things you did made an impact on different disciples. Just like them, I will notice things that other people don't notice, and other people will notice things that I don't notice. Help me to be open to learning from other people and help me to share what I know with them too.

Sailor's Log

Draw this scene of Jesus calling the fishermen the way you imagine it. Include yourself in the scene—where are you standing?

DAY 18

Deep Dive

This telling of the story leaves out a lot of details, but it does focus on one thing really strongly. It shows us that when Jesus called Simon, Andrew, James, and John, they left everything *immediately*: their jobs, their stuff, their homes, their friends, and even their families.

It's hard to be the first one to do something. Simon, Andrew, James, and John were the first ones out of all the people they knew to be called to follow Jesus. This must have been really scary! They were following a teacher that they didn't know very well, and they didn't know anyone else following him either. They were leaving behind everything and everyone they did know to follow Jesus. But they went, even though their family and friends weren't already following Jesus. They went first. Because of this, they became missionaries. They ended up bringing their family, friends, and strangers to Jesus to be saved.

John, the youngest of these four fishermen, wrote in his Gospel these words of Jesus: "You did not choose me, but I chose you" (John 15:16). Jesus chose his disciples before any of them even knew him, because he knew, loved, and trusted them.

FACT: In 2011, a man in Brazil found a Magellanic penguin in trouble. The penguin was covered in oil and was going to die. The man chose to rescue it. He cleaned it off and nursed it back to health, then set it free. But for years the grateful penguin loyally returned to visit the man.

When Jesus chose his disciples, they knew they didn't deserve to be chosen—they knew he did it only out of love for them, and not because of anything they had done right. Because of this, they were so grateful for his love that they chose to follow Jesus through everything. Jesus chose them, and they chose Jesus.

Jesus has chosen you too.

When we are baptized, we officially become Christians. Christians are people who follow Jesus Christ. And Jesus Christ has a mission—to bring everyone to God. We follow him on that mission, so we become missionaries. He is calling you to be a missionary, just as he called the fishermen.

How does it feel to know that Jesus has actually chosen you to be a missionary? What does this inspire in you?

Prayer Prompt

Lord Jesus, you call the people you choose to go out and bring the Gospel to the whole world. Where is it that you are asking me to bring you today? Please help me notice where and when you are nudging me to share you today.

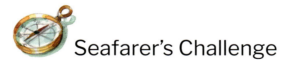

Seafarer's Challenge

Think of one way that you can be a missionary to the people around you in everyday life. Then think of one way that you can be a missionary to people far away. Pray about which one God might want you to try right now. (Maybe it is both!) When you feel like God is nudging you in one direction (or both directions) follow him there today.

After John the Baptist Dies

Herod had arrested John, bound him, and put him in prison. . . . He commanded . . . and had John beheaded in the prison. The head was brought on a platter and given to the girl, who brought it to her mother. His disciples came and took the body and buried it; then they went and told Jesus. Now when Jesus heard this, he withdrew from there in a boat to a deserted place by himself. But when the crowds heard it, they followed him on foot from the towns. When he went ashore, he saw a great crowd; and he had compassion for them and cured their sick.

Matthew 14:3, 9–14

DAY 19
Setting Sail

Jesus' cousin John was an amazing man. Jesus and John the Baptist shared a very special bond. In the Gospel of Luke, we read that they were born less than a year apart. When they were still just fetuses, John leaped in his mother's womb the first time Mary came close to him with Jesus in her womb. Because of the Holy Spirit, John could sense Jesus' presence even as a fetus, and he was full of joy to have his cousin and Savior near him.

When the two boys grew up, John started preaching first. He prepared people to open their hearts to what Jesus would have to say, and who Jesus was. When Jesus came to John to be baptized, John told him he wasn't worthy to baptize him, because John knew that he himself was a sinner and Jesus was not. But Jesus reassured John and told him it was okay, asking him to baptize him anyway. When Jesus began preaching, many of John's followers left the Baptist to follow Jesus. But John wasn't upset—he *wanted* his friends to follow Jesus! John gave his whole life for people to get to know and love his precious cousin.

John was very special to Jesus, and Jesus felt his cousin's death deeply. It was like being wounded inside. Jesus needed to step away from teaching for a bit, because he needed to be alone. He needed to mourn.

At some point, we all lose someone we love. It's a scary thing to have to face someone's death. And it is very painful to go through. When we lose someone we love, it's hard to keep going as if everything were still normal. We need time to mourn.

Mourning is natural when we lose someone or something important to us.

FACT: Even sea mammals mourn. Mother dolphins have been seen carrying their dead calves for weeks. In 2018, one orca pushed the body of her dead calf for 1,000 miles before she was ready to let it go.

We need time to not be okay. Sometimes we feel the pain right away. Other times we don't feel the pain until later. But no matter when the pain hits us, we need time to grieve. Grieving can involve a lot of emotions. We might feel sad, lonely, angry, tired, or depressed. We might feel scared or anxious. Or we might be overcome by numbness and not really feel anything at all. We might have moments when we remember great things about the person we lost and end up laughing and smiling even as we cry. And by the end, even if we are still sad, we feel peace when we entrust our loved one to Jesus, who loves them even more than we do.

Jesus knows what it is like to mourn. He cried and mourned too. When we lose someone important to us, we have to admit that we are not okay. When we do, we are free to step into that boat with Jesus. He lets us be sad and cry with him, and he even mourns with us. It's important to mourn, but don't mourn alone. Mourn with Jesus—he understands better than anyone.

Prayer Prompt

Think of someone you loved, knew, or know about who has passed away. Say this prayer for them, asking God to take care of them forever in heaven: "Eternal rest grant to them, O Lord, and may eternal light shine on them. May they rest in peace. Amen."

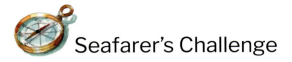 ## Seafarer's Challenge

God teaches us in the Bible that we can pray for people who have passed away. The next time you visit or drive past a graveyard, say a prayer for the people who are buried there and for their families.

DAY 20

Deep Dive

We all have times in our life when things go wrong. Depending on what is happening, we might need to be with people, or we might need time alone.

Sometimes we try to be alone, but then someone interrupts us because they need something. When this happens, it can be really easy to get annoyed or angry and lash out at that person. It can be hard to shift our focus from our own hurt to the need of someone else. But even though we all do need some time alone, and it's okay to say so, we can also learn how to consider the needs of others. Even when we are hurting, we can help others heal.

FACT: When a sea otter pup dies, its mother is often very confused and sad. But mother sea otters who have lost a pup might also adopt an orphan pup. In some aquariums, baby otters that have been rescued are put in a pool with a mother sea otter who has no pup of her own, either because her pup died or because her pup grew up and left. Often, that mother will adopt the orphaned baby and care for it until it is ready to be released into the wild. Her instinct is to be generous, even if she had a loss before, and her generosity saves another pup's life.

Jesus shows us how to be generous and caring even when we are hurting. He was in a lot of pain because his cousin had just died. He had sailed across the sea to be alone. And he did need time to be alone and mourn. But he didn't let that stop him from caring about the people who needed him and were waiting for him on the other shore. He healed and taught them, then he took time later to be alone, mourn, and pray. And his generosity made a big difference in the lives of every single person that he healed.

When we are down, we don't have to let it stop us from loving other people. We still need time to take care of ourselves, but not in a way that shuts out other people. We can be kind to others even when we are hurting. And that can make a big difference in their lives.

Prayer Prompt

Lord Jesus, you know what it feels like to want to be alone. But you also know how to love people, even when you are hurting. Give me the strength to be kind and generous when I am hurting. And help me to remember to make time to take care of myself too.

Sailor's Log

Write about or draw a time when you really needed to be alone. Ask yourself if you were still open to listening to and loving other people. Write down a goal of how you can be more generous with people the next time you are hurting, while still taking time to care for yourself.

Jesus and Peter Walk on Water

Immediately he made the disciples get into the boat and go on ahead to the other side, while he dismissed the crowds. And after he had dismissed the crowds, he went up the mountain by himself to pray. When evening came, he was there alone, but by this time the boat, battered by the waves, was far from the land, for the wind was against them. And early in the morning he came walking toward them on the sea. But when the disciples saw him walking on the sea, they were terrified, saying, "It is a ghost!" And they cried out in fear. But immediately Jesus spoke to them and said, "Take heart, it is I; do not be afraid."

    Peter answered him, "Lord, if it is you, command me to come to you on the water." He said, "Come." So Peter got out of the boat, started walking on the water, and came toward Jesus. But when he noticed the strong wind, he became frightened, and beginning to sink, he cried out, "Lord, save me!" Jesus immediately reached out his hand and caught him, saying to him, "You of little faith, why did you doubt?" When they got into the boat, the wind ceased. And those in the boat worshiped him, saying, "Truly you are the Son of God."

Matthew 14: 22–33

DAY 21
Setting Sail

In pictures of this scene, Jesus is standing far from the boat, and Peter is making his way over to Jesus. But there is a big hint in this story that tells us that's probably not what happened. Look back at the story. Can you spot it?

If you've ever seen a storm on the water with high winds and crashing waves, you know that storms are LOUD. You have to scream into the ear of the person beside you for them to hear anything you're saying. Storms on the Sea of Galilee get really bad.

> **FACT**: In March 1992, there was a particularly bad storm on this same sea with sixty-mile-per-hour winds sending ten-foot waves crashing into the town of Tiberias, causing significant damage. The waves even broke into a hotel, but the owner said there was a positive side: the crashing waves threw fish into the hotel, so he didn't have to buy any to serve for lunch!

In a storm like this, if Peter and the disciples could hear anything Jesus was saying, and if Jesus could hear Peter, then they all had to be very close to each other. Jesus was probably quite close to the boat. So when Peter stepped out onto the water, Jesus would not have been far from him.

But even though Jesus was standing right in front of him, Peter still forgot him! He got so distracted by the wind and waves that he forgot that Jesus was literally right there. When he looked away from Jesus and focused only on the storm, he started to sink.

But Peter did remember one thing—he remembered to call out to the only person who could save him. Jesus was right there, and he caught Peter before the waves could suck him under.

We can wonder why Peter got scared of the storm when Jesus was standing on the water right in front of him. It seems like such a silly mistake! But if we look at our own lives, we sometimes do the same thing. In everything scary, hurtful, confusing, or tragic in our lives, Jesus is literally right beside us. But just like Peter, we focus on the things happening around us instead of on Jesus. We feel scared, lonely, or overwhelmed. We don't think about praying; we don't think to tell God how we feel and ask him for help; we don't think to read Jesus' words to us in Scripture; and we don't think about going to church and kneeling or sitting there to be with Jesus present in the Eucharist. We forget that he is standing with us in the midst of the storm.

But even if we forget, that doesn't change the fact that Jesus is still right there. He is not sinking. He won't let us sink either. Like Peter, we just need to call out to him for help. We can pray in our own words. We can meet him in the Bible. We can sit with him in church. He will always, always catch us.

Is there a storm in your life that makes you anxious and takes your eyes off of Jesus when he can help you? Or do you know someone who is going through a storm and can't see Jesus in it? What can you say to Jesus today to ask his help in this situation? Tell him what hurts the most, ask him to help you . . . and thank him, because even if the storm keeps blowing, you know he is not going to let you get sucked under. His grip is strong and firm, and he is holding on to you, because he loves you.

Prayer Prompt

Jesus, right now I have a lot of anxiety about this situation with _____ _____. I keep forgetting to look at you and hold on to you, because I keep worrying about _____. So, I am asking you for help. Help me to trust you. Help me to believe that no matter how loud the storm gets, or how wet I get from the waves crashing around me, you are going to get me through this. Help me to be kind even when I am afraid, and to trust you even if my body and mind feel nervous. I know you are right here. Thank you for holding on to me. Thank you for promising me that you won't let me fall. I want to always remember to rely on you. I know I am safe with you.

Seafarer's Challenge—Express Yourself

What does it look like for Jesus to be beside you in this storm in your life? (Create a picture, poem, emoji, etc.)

DAY 22

Deep Dive

This was a big storm, the kind that pitched you back and forth with no break to catch your breath—you had to keep going, no matter how you or your body felt. You had to keep going to stay alive.

People react to situations differently. Our minds, emotions, and bodies react differently. Have you ever felt motion-sick before? Some people never get motion-sick in cars, planes, or boats. But for some people, the rocking motion of a little boat in a storm is too much for their bodies to handle.

> **FACT**: Seasickness happens when your inner ear, which helps your body keep your balance, registers up-and-down motion from the waves, but your eye, which also helps your body keep its balance, registers your surroundings as looking steadier. Your brain gets stressed by two opposite signals and puts out a distress-call to your body that can lead to vomiting.

Many of the disciples were fishermen, including Peter, so they were used to the pitching of the waves. But not all the disciples were.

There are many icons of the storm at sea described in the Gospels. In most versions, you can see the disciples struggling not to capsize, waving for help, or even trying not to lose their fishing net. But in one peculiar version, all the disciples in the boat are struggling to stay afloat in the strong wind . . . except for one. That disciple can be seen leaning over the edge of the boat, about to puke.

Of course, Scripture doesn't tell us if anyone got seasick. But it's likely that at some point, someone had to lean over the side of the boat and empty his stomach. If a disciple did have to vomit when Peter stepped out on the water, he might have actually missed the entire miracle! He might have been so busy puking that he didn't see what happened!

You probably won't be seasick on a boat while Jesus strolls by on the waves. But there will be times in your life that Jesus is trying to show you something, or is working a miracle around you, and you are too distracted to notice. Maybe you're distracted by things happening around you and forget to take time to pray, or you're distracted by feeling anxious about something, and you miss seeing what God is doing in your life.

When that disciple stopped puking and lifted his head to see what was going on, Jesus and Peter might already have been back in the boat. That disciple couldn't have known what happened unless the other disciples told him. He had to listen to what they had seen and experienced. But when the others shared what they had seen, the sick disciple would learn something new about Jesus, and learn to trust him in a way that could change his life.

Just like the disciples, it's important for us to share something about God when we think it could help someone know and love God better. And just like the poor seasick disciple, it is important for us to listen to people's stories about God's amazing power and love when they share them. We can learn a lot about God's faithfulness and love that way, and it can help us understand how he loves us too.

Prayer Prompt

Think of someone you wish could really get to know God better. Maybe it's a friend, a family member, or a neighbor. Ask God, in your own words, that they may come to know him, and ask God if he wants to use you to help that happen!

Seafarer's Challenge

If you know someone who is feeling down, they might feel so bad that they miss seeing what Jesus is doing in their lives. Help them to see that he's there: tell them, in person or on social media, that you are praying for them today. It might feel awkward at first, but you may be surprised how much it could mean to the other person.

Jesus Asleep in the Boat

When evening had come, he said to them, "Let us go across to the other side." And leaving the crowd behind, they took him with them in the boat, just as he was. Other boats were with him. A great windstorm arose, and the waves beat into the boat, so that the boat was already being swamped. But he was in the stern, asleep on the cushion; and they woke him up and said to him, "Teacher, do you not care that we are perishing?" He woke up and rebuked the wind, and said to the sea, "Peace! Be still!" Then the wind ceased, and there was a dead calm. He said to them, "Why are you afraid? Have you still no faith?" And they were filled with great awe and said to one another, "Who then is this, that even the wind and the sea obey him?"

Mark 4:35–41

DAY 23
Setting Sail

"Do you not care?!"

It seems like a really rude thing to say to Jesus. He was literally exhausting himself by walking from town to town, caring for the sick, teaching crowds, praying into the night, and making sure the disciples were getting along well together. And, although the disciples didn't know this, he was preparing to do the hardest thing anyone can do for someone else—he was getting ready to give up his life for us, dying in a really horrible and torturous way. How could the disciples think he didn't care?

But we can be like that too. The disciples didn't see Jesus doing anything to save them from drowning, and they assumed he didn't care, even though everything he had done before that should have told them that he did care—a lot! When things are going wrong for us, sometimes we think God doesn't care, even though everything he has done before should tell us that he does!

FACT: Baby sea lions spend a lot of time not being able to see their mothers. A few days after a baby sea lion is born, its mother leaves it to go find food. Her baby can't see her doing anything, but she is working hard to make sure her baby is well fed. Later, the mother sea lion has to teach her baby how to swim. At first the mother stays close by in the water, but then she starts to go farther away. Soon, the baby sea lion can't see its mother anymore, but she is still watching carefully to make sure her baby is okay.

When we don't see God at work in our lives, we sometimes wonder if he even cares. But when we look at the cross, we remember that God does care . . . he cares more than anyone. Having faith means trusting that he cares about us more than we can ever understand.

What is something that can help you remember how much God cares for you? Is it looking at a crucifix, going to Mass, wearing a cross necklace or a rosary bracelet, thinking about what God says in Scripture, or recalling good memories? Think of one thing today that reminds you how much God cares.

Prayer Prompt

Lord, when I don't see you doing anything, help me to remember how much you care. I know I can talk to you about whatever is going on with me—thank you for thinking that it is important. Thanks for always being there for me, and for giving your life for me.

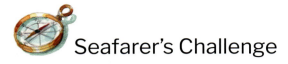# Seafarer's Challenge

    Is there someone in your life who might need to be reminded of how much God cares about them? What is one thing you could say or do for them that would help them remember? Find a chance to do it for them to let them know how much they are loved by God.

DAY 24
Deep Dive

If their boat was filling up with water, it's amazing that Jesus slept through it. He must have been exhausted from everything he had been doing before they boarded the boat.

Jesus is the Son of God made man. He is fully Divine, and he is fully human. As humans, we aren't a soul that happens to have a body, and we aren't a body that happens to have a soul: we are our body and we are our soul, together. When Jesus became man to save us, he came to save our body and soul. He saves our souls from the penalty of our sins, and he saves our bodies through the resurrection of the body. He wants to save the whole of us, body and soul. He knows what it is to be a soul and body.

> **FACT**: 71 percent of the earth's surface is covered with water. This percentage is almost exactly the same as the two most important parts of our bodies—the human heart and the human brain are 73 percent water.

This reminds us that our bodies were not created by accident. God made us as an important part of creation. We can look at creation to help us understand some things about ourselves. But God also tells us that we have to look beyond creation to him if we want to understand *everything* about ourselves.

Our body is how we are able to interact with other people. Others can know us only through our bodies. Our bodies enable us to love other people—our smile, our hug, our helpful gestures are all ways of loving with our body.

But we can also struggle with our body. We might not like the way we look, or we might get sick or tired when we are trying to do something important. All people have special gifts because of their bodies: the abilities God gives them, the biological sex God gives them, the unique face God gives them. All people also have limitations because of their bodies: things they can't do or things they are not comfortable with.

Jesus shows us how to live in our bodies. He shows us how to love God and other people with our bodies. Jesus used his body when he prayed, and he touched other people to let them know they were not alone. He shows us how to accept and deal with the limitations of our bodies. He knew when it was good not to eat and when it was important to eat, he knew when he could push himself hard and when he had to sleep. He shows us how to accept and take care of our bodies—after all, they are a gift from God!

Have you ever thought about how you are both your soul and your body together? Taking care of your body and using it to help other people shows God you are grateful for the gift of life. How are you taking care of your body today?

Prayer Prompt

Lord Jesus, you took on a human body when you came into the Virgin Mary's womb. You had to learn how to walk and talk. You had growing pains. Your arms got sore from working hard. You got injured. You got hungry and tired. You smiled and laughed and hugged people and danced. You probably looked like your mom. You know what it's like to be soul and body. Help me to love every part of the body you gave me. Help me to learn why you gave me my face, my gender, my special abilities. Help me accept my limitations and learn to deal with them in a healthy way. And thank you—thank you for making me, me.

 ## Sailor's Log

What is something about your body that you are very grateful for? Write it down and explain why you are thankful to God for this gift. What is something that you struggle to accept? Write it down and ask God to help you understand this part of yourself.

Jesus Gets Frustrated

The Pharisees came and began to argue with him, asking him for a sign from heaven, to test him. And he sighed deeply in his spirit and said, "Why does this generation ask for a sign? Truly I tell you, no sign will be given to this generation." And he left them, and getting into the boat again, he went across to the other side.

   Now the disciples had forgotten to bring any bread; and they had only one loaf with them in the boat. And he cautioned them, saying, "Watch out—beware of the yeast of the Pharisees and the yeast of Herod." They said to one another, "It is because we have no bread." And becoming aware of it, Jesus said to them, "Why are you talking about having no bread? Do you still not perceive or understand? Are your hearts hardened? Do you have eyes, and fail to see? Do you have ears, and fail to hear? And do you not remember? When I broke the five loaves for the five thousand, how many baskets full of broken pieces did you collect?" They said to him, "Twelve." "And the seven for the four thousand, how many baskets full of broken pieces did you collect?" And they said to him, "Seven." Then he said to them, "Do you not yet understand?"

Mark 8:11–21

DAY 25
Setting Sail

Thirteen hungry men in a boat does not equal a fun ride. That's probably what the disciples were busy blaming themselves for when Jesus decided to use the thing on their mind—bread—to warn them about the Pharisees. The disciples didn't get it at first, and we can be confused right along with them. To understand what Jesus was saying, we have to know about packing food for boat trips, and about how bread is made.

> **FACT**: Sailors from different cultures packed different foods for different kinds of journeys. When Polynesian sailors went exploring, they would bring coconuts. The coconuts could be towed in the water without spoiling, so they took up no room on the boat, plus they provided both food and water. For short trips in Israel, sailors would pack bread, because it was easy to carry, light, filling, gave the sailors carbs and energy, and was easy to find.

But bread couldn't be made on board, only carried. Bread making had two important steps that being at sea made impossible. The first was using yeast for the bread to rise. The second was making a fire for the bread to cook.

Yeast is technically a kind of fungus—like mushrooms, but very small. When you put live yeast in baking, it makes your bread rise so that it is soft and fluffy and give it a delicious flavor. (But don't worry, cooking the bread kills the yeast so it isn't alive when you eat it!) Good yeast will make your bread rise. But if you use bad yeast, which is yeast that has already died, nothing will happen—your bread will not rise, and you will end up with a super thick cracker to break your teeth on, and no bread to eat.

When Jesus said to beware the yeast of the Pharisees, he meant that the example the Pharisees were giving was like bad yeast—it might look okay at first, but if you try to live it out it won't help you at all. Just the way bad yeast leaves you with a tooth-breaking cracker, what the Pharisees were doing could not help people get closer to God. Jesus was telling his disciples that if they started thinking and acting like the Pharisees, they wouldn't be able to help other people or become closer to God themselves.

We have to be careful about what kind of "yeast" we are using in our lives too. Are we following the example of people who seem popular and happy on the outside but actually can't bring us closer to God? Or are we following the example of people who can bring us closer to God, so that we can in turn help other people and rise to new life ourselves?

Prayer Prompt

Lord Jesus, there are some people I really look up to, like _____ and _____. Help me to take an honest look at whether they are really helping me get closer to you and teaching me to love other people better. I want to follow you before I follow anyone else, because I know you want to raise me to new life. Help me to follow you more closely today.

Sailor's Log

Write down the names of two to five people you look up to or admire. Write a prayer for each one of them, asking God to be with them and to help them be open to getting to know his love more.

DAY 26

Deep Dive

This passage is actually kind of funny. If Jesus ever face-palmed in the Gospels, it was probably here.

The disciples are wrapped up in thinking about how they forgot to pack bread for the boat ride. Since they are all thinking of bread anyway, Jesus uses the process of making bread as a way to explain the danger of thinking like the Pharisees. Actually, it's a perfect way to explain it, but the disciples literally have zero clue as to what Jesus is talking about.

> **FACT**: Moray eels are always opening and closing their mouths. Unlike most fish, moray eels don't have gill covers on their sides to get oxygen to their inside gills, so they have to use their mouths to pump water to their inside gills to breathe. Their chomping mouth is actually communicating life, but some divers who are focused on looking for danger have no clue what it really means and assume the eel wants to bite them.

If those divers swam back and watched carefully, they would realize that the moray eel always chomps its mouth, even when there is no one around. But often divers don't watch carefully enough to understand.

That's what happened here with the disciples. If they had taken a step back and thought about what had just happened with the Pharisees, who were refusing to listen to Jesus unless he worked dramatic signs, they would have realized that Jesus wasn't talking about buying yeast or bread from the Pharisees—he was warning his disciples not to follow what the Pharisees were doing and thinking. But no one thought about what had happened just before they boarded the boat, because they were so distracted by their hungry tummies. So no one understood.

We too can have trouble understanding what Jesus says, especially when we read the Bible. Sometimes we don't understand a story in the Bible because there is a mystery in it that Jesus will help us to solve over time. But sometimes it's because we aren't paying attention to the clues. When this happens, it's important to step back and look for clues. What happened in the verses just before the story we are reading? Or are there notes in our Bible that give the cultural context of what's going on? Many times, if we know what led up to the story we are looking at, we can understand it better. We can also read the verses that come just after the story, in case they can give us some clues. Or, if Jesus is quoting a psalm from the Old Testament, we can flip to that psalm and see what it says. If none of that helps, we can ask a priest we trust to explain it using different words that can help us understand.

Prayer Prompt

Lord Jesus, to be honest, I don't always understand what you're talking about when I read your words in the Gospels. Sometimes I don't understand other parts of the Bible either. Help me to stay calm when I am confused about your words to me, and to keep watching for clues as to what you mean. I want to understand you, the way you understand me.

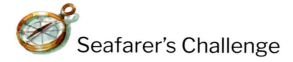 Seafarer's Challenge

Pick up a Bible and open to one of the four Gospels (according to Matthew, Mark, Luke, or John). Choose one story to read that does not take place on the sea. What does Jesus say or do in this story? Does it make sense to you? If it does, great! If it doesn't, see if you can find the clues to help you understand.

Hail, Our Only Hope

Save us, O Christ our Savior, through the power of your cross.
You who saved Peter on the sea, have mercy on us.

After the Resurrection: Sea of Tiberias

After these things Jesus showed himself again to the disciples by the Sea of Tiberias; and he showed himself in this way. Gathered there together were Simon Peter, Thomas called the Twin, Nathanael of Cana in Galilee, the sons of Zebedee, and two others of his disciples. Simon Peter said to them, "I am going fishing." They said to him, "We will go with you." They went out and got into the boat, but that night they caught nothing.

Just after daybreak, Jesus stood on the beach; but the disciples did not know that it was Jesus. Jesus said to them, "Children, you have no fish, have you?" They answered him, "No." He said to them, "Cast the net to the right side of the boat, and you will find some." So they cast it, and now they were not able to haul it in because there were so many fish. That disciple whom Jesus loved said to Peter, "It is the Lord!" When Simon Peter heard that it was the Lord, he put on some clothes, for he was naked, and jumped into the sea. But the other disciples came in the boat, dragging the net full of fish, for they were not far from the land, only about a hundred yards off.

When they had gone ashore, they saw a charcoal fire there, with fish on it, and bread. Jesus said to them, "Bring some of the fish that you have just caught." So Simon Peter went aboard and hauled the net ashore, full of large fish, a hundred fifty-three of them; and though there were so many, the net was not torn. Jesus said to them, "Come and have breakfast." Now none of the disciples dared to ask him, "Who are you?" because they knew it was the Lord. Jesus came and took the bread and gave it to them, and did the same with the fish. This was now the third time that Jesus appeared to the disciples after he was raised from the dead. When they had finished breakfast, Jesus said to Simon Peter, "Simon son of John, do you love me more than these?" He said to him, "Yes, Lord; you know that I love you." Jesus said to him, "Feed my lambs." A second time he said to him, "Simon son of John, do you love me?" He said to him, "Yes, Lord; you know that I love you." Jesus said to him, "Tend my sheep." He said to him the third time, "Simon son of John, do you love me?" Peter felt hurt because he said to him the third time, "Do you love me?" And he said to him, "Lord, you know everything; you know that I love you." Jesus said to him, "Feed my sheep."

John 21:1–17

DAY 27
Setting Sail

This is the background for the event you just read about: Jesus had died on the cross. Even though he was the person who had saved the disciples on the sea and changed their lives, the person whom they loved, he had been brutally killed. The disciples had all run away and hidden—except John. John was the only man brave enough to stay with Jesus as he was dying. He stood there alongside Mary Magdalene, a few other women, and Mary, Jesus' mother.

It was as if the world had fallen apart. The disciples had thought Jesus would be the man to save Israel, but now he was gone.

Then, on the third day, Jesus had risen from the dead. He really had saved the disciples—from sin and from death! After that, he had sent them back to the Sea of Tiberias—also called the Sea of Galilee—saying he would see them soon. After that he had disappeared.

In Galilee, Peter decided to go fishing. The others went with him. After a bad night of fishing, a stranger told them to put their nets out again, and they caught more than their boat could hold.

Does this story seem familiar? It was exactly what had happened the very first time Jesus had worked a miracle for Peter, Andrew, James, and John.

It seems like Peter was in shock. He was standing there in the boat, amazed, in his underwear (when they were working really hard, men would take their tunics off to cool down). But John remembered. He and Peter had seen this before! That's why John grabbed Peter and said, "It's the Lord!"

FACT: Whales and dolphins have fantastic memories. Recent studies suggest that when blue whales migrate in the ocean looking for food and places to raise their babies, they might actually be using their memories, not other kinds of instincts, to find the best places! They go back to places that were good before to find what they need now, because they can remember those places.

There are so many times in the Bible that God asks us to remember. It's easy for us to forget him. But when we take time to remember him and everything he has done, it helps us to trust and love him better. Sometimes, when we are having trouble remembering, God will bring a memory back. A song that reminds us of him might randomly come up in a playlist. We might open our Bible to a verse we used to really love. We might walk past a house that has a religious picture in the window or pass a car with a bumper sticker of a fish. God uses all kinds of things to help us remember him.

What important memories do you have of God in your life? If you can't think of any in your own life, what do you remember God doing in the life of someone you know?

 Prayer Prompt

Lord, I want to remember the amazing things you have done, so that I can trust you better and love you better every day. But, to be honest, I don't always remember you. Forgive me for the times I forget you. Help me to remember you more often, and to thank you for everything you have done for me. I want to live with a grateful heart.

Sailor's Log

Think back over your whole life. Start writing down every moment that you remember knowing God was there. These might be things that happened to you or a loved one, things people told you about, or things you read in the Bible that left an impact on you. When you have made your list, highlight three to five things you never want to forget. Why are they especially important to you?

DAY 28

Deep Dive

When Jesus was arrested and put on trial, only John and Peter stayed. Peter wanted to be there to support Jesus. But when someone recognized Peter as one of Jesus' disciples, Peter got scared that he might get in trouble too. Three times he told everyone nearby that he had nothing to do with Jesus. He denied the person he loved most in the whole world. When he realized what he had done, he felt so bad that he ran away, broke down, and cried.

That is why, as Jesus was dying on the cross, John was the only man standing with the group of women who were there for Jesus. Peter let his feelings of shame matter more to him than knowing that Jesus might feel alone on the cross. He let something in his life matter more than Jesus.

But this time by the Sea of Tiberias is different. When John realizes that the stranger on the shore is Jesus, everyone stays in the boat to keep hold of the fish they caught—except Peter. This time, Peter doesn't let anything matter more than Jesus—not the fish, not the boat, not staying dry, not looking cool—he throws his tunic back on and plunges into the water to get to Jesus as fast as he can. Jesus gave up everything for love of Peter, dying to save him. Now Peter is ready to give up everything for Jesus.

FACT: When a mother octopus lays her eggs, she stops going out to find food in order to care for the eggs. She protects the eggs and helps them grow. Different types of octopus have to wait

for different timeframes for their eggs to hatch. The longest wait on record belongs to the type of deep-sea octopus called *Graneledone boreopacifica*. In 2007, researchers tracked a single *Graneledone boreopacifica* octopus guarding her eggs for fifty-three months straight—from 2007 to 2011! When her eggs finally hatched, the mother octopus died from starvation. She had given her whole life to save her babies.

Jesus gave his whole life for Peter, even when Peter wasn't ready to give his life to Jesus. But now that Peter was ready, do you notice what Jesus did? He asked Peter three times, "Do you love me?" This way he gave Peter a chance to make up for the three times he denied Jesus. Even though it was hard for Peter to be reminded of what he had done, he was able to say "yes." And in turn, Jesus entrusted Peter with the care of all the people who followed him.

When we let anything matter more to us than Jesus, we turn our back on the person who loves us most. But when we realize just how much Jesus loves us—so much that he died a horrible death to save us—we can't help loving him back. He gave us his whole life. When we realize just what that means, we are inspired to give him our whole life back.

Are there parts of your life that you are holding back from Jesus? Things that you let matter more than him, or things you don't invite him into? How can you change that today?

Prayer Prompt

Lord Jesus, how can I ever love you enough? How can I ever repay what you have done for me? I can't—but you don't want me to repay you. You just want me. Help me to love you with my whole heart and my whole life. I want to live for you.

Seafarer's Challenge

Take some time to look at a crucifix. Remember how far Jesus went for love of you. And remember that the cross was not the end—he didn't just die for you, he rose again and conquered death for you, so that you can live with him forever! Think of one way you want to show Jesus your gratitude for this and do it today.

Acts of the Apostles: Paul's Shipwreck

When it was decided that we were to sail for Italy, they transferred Paul and some other prisoners to a centurion of the Augustan Cohort, named Julius. . . .

Since much time had been lost and sailing was now dangerous, because even the Fast had already gone by, Paul advised them, saying, "Sirs, I can see that the voyage will be with danger and much heavy loss, not only of the cargo and the ship, but also of our lives." But the centurion paid more attention to the pilot and to the owner of the ship than to what Paul said. Since the harbor was not suitable for spending the winter, the majority was in favor of putting to sea from there, on the chance that somehow they could reach Phoenix, where they could spend the winter. It was a harbor of Crete, facing southwest and northwest.

When a moderate south wind began to blow, they thought they could achieve their purpose; so they weighed anchor and began to sail past Crete, close to the shore. But soon a violent wind, called the northeaster, rushed down from Crete. . . . We were being pounded by the storm so violently that on the next day they began to throw the cargo overboard, and on the third day with their own hands they threw the ship's tackle overboard. When neither sun nor stars appeared for many days, and no small tempest raged, all hope of our being saved was at last abandoned.

Paul then stood up among them and said, "Men, you should have listened to me and not have set sail from Crete and thereby avoided this damage and loss. I urge you now to keep up your courage, for there will be no loss of life among you, but only of the ship. For last night there stood by me an angel of the God to whom I belong and whom I worship, and he said, 'Do not be afraid, Paul; you must stand before the emperor; and indeed, God has granted safety to all those who are sailing with you.' So keep up your courage, men, for I have faith in God that it will be exactly as I have been told. But we will have to run aground on some island."

When the fourteenth night had come, as we were drifting across the sea of Adria, about midnight the sailors suspected that they were nearing land. So they took soundings and found twenty fathoms; a little farther on they took soundings again and found fifteen fathoms. Fearing that we might run on the rocks, they let down four anchors from the stern and prayed for day to come. . . .

Just before daybreak, Paul urged all of them to take some food, saying, "Today is the fourteenth day that you have been in suspense and remaining without food, having eaten nothing. Therefore I urge you to take some food, for it will help you survive; for none of you will lose a hair from your heads." After he had said this, he took bread; and giving thanks to God in the presence of all, he broke it and began to eat. Then all of them were encouraged and took food for themselves. (We were in all two hundred seventy-six persons in the ship.) After they had satisfied their hunger, they lightened the ship by throwing the wheat into the sea.

In the morning they did not recognize the land, but they noticed a bay with a beach, on which they planned to run the ship ashore, if they could. So they cast off the anchors and left them in the sea. At the same time they loosened the ropes that tied the steering-oars; then hoisting the foresail to the wind, they made for the beach. But striking a reef, they ran the ship aground; the bow stuck and remained immovable, but the stern was being broken up by the force of the waves. The soldiers' plan was to kill the prisoners, so that none might swim away and escape; but the centurion, wishing to save Paul, kept them from carrying out their plan. He ordered those who could swim to jump overboard first and make for the land, and the rest to follow, some on planks and others on pieces of the ship. And so it was that all were brought safely to land.

Acts 27: 1, 9–14, 18–20, 21–29, 33–44

DAY 29

Setting Sail

Paul was a Pharisee who had been putting followers of Jesus in jail because he thought they were wrong about Jesus being the Messiah. But then the resurrected Jesus had appeared to him, revealing his true identity. After that, Paul had dedicated his whole life to making sure everyone in the world could get the chance to meet Jesus too. But in his travels he got into trouble and was eventually arrested for preaching about Jesus.

Now it seems that Paul is somewhere he shouldn't have to be. He has done nothing wrong and is unjustly being held prisoner. Someone who has done nothing wrong wouldn't normally be in chains on a storm-tossed boat in the middle of the Mediterranean Sea. But by the end of the story, we realize that was actually exactly where Paul needed to be.

FACT: A "Blue Grotto" is a coastal cave full of water with an opening you can barely squeeze through to get inside from the open water. Inside, instead of sunlight coming in through the roof as it might do normally, there is an opening below the water that lets light in when the sun reaches the right angle in the sky. When the light floods through the underwater open-

> ing, the water absorbs the long wavelength light (warm colors) and lets through short wavelength light (blue). So as the light passes through the water and up onto the dry walls, the walls of the cave are bathed in a magical blue light! Visitors can wait in a boat on the water inside the cave for the sun to hit the right spot so they can witness this amazing phenomenon.

The light coming from this unexpected place changes everything about the cave and makes it into one of the most breathtaking caves on earth . . . all because the opening for the light is somewhere it wouldn't normally be.

Paul is like that opening. On board a prisoner ship, there isn't supposed to be an innocent person, let alone someone who is a messenger of God's grace and salvation. People like that are supposed to be in places of religious worship. But here, Paul's openness to God allows God's words to rescue all those on the ship, making everyone realize the beauty of who Paul's God is. With the determination of a Christian unafraid of death, because he knows about the resurrection, Paul saves everyone on board the ship by reminding the sailors of their duty.

Maybe Paul shouldn't have been a prisoner. But he needed to be on that ship to save everyone else, and to introduce them to the God who loved them. And that's exactly what he did.

Sometimes we get trapped in unfair situations—we get in trouble for something we didn't do, or we don't get a grade we earned, or we have to clean up after someone else's mess. In situations we can't get out of, we can ask God to help us stay open to his love, so we can be openings for his light to shine in. Things might not all work out perfectly, but in these times we can really start to introduce people to our loving God. We want God to shine through us so unexpectedly that everyone is stunned by how beautiful he is, just like the first time someone saw the blue glow light up that dark, gloomy cave.

Prayer Prompt

Lord, when I am in an unfair situation, I usually get angry. I know it's not bad to feel angry about something unfair, but I don't want to get stuck in my anger. I want to bring you into the situation to change things and remind people of what it means to live as people who believe in the resurrection. And help me remember too.

Seafarer's Challenge

Look at some pictures of Blue Grottos. Think of two ways that you can bring beauty and light into unexpected places in your life. Try to do at least one of them this week.

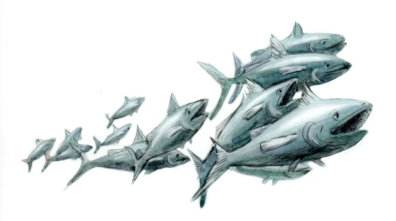

DAY 30
Deep Dive

Open your Bible and take a peek at 2 Corinthians 11:25 (Paul's second letter to the Church in Corinth). In it, we find out that Paul didn't get shipwrecked only once—he actually survived THREE shipwrecks AND was lost adrift at sea for twenty-four hours. After he describes these and many other awful experiences, Paul says, "Who is weak, and I am not weak?" And a little further on, he writes, "[The Lord] said to me, 'My grace is sufficient for you, for power is made perfect in weakness'" (2 Corinthians 11:29; 12:9).

We don't know all of the weaknesses that Paul struggled with, just as not everyone can tell every weakness that we ourselves struggle with. But after so many accidents at sea, it wouldn't be surprising if Paul had developed a fear of the water. This can happen to anyone who has a dangerous experience at sea.

> **FACT**: Thalassophobia is the official name of a serious fear of the ocean or any deep water. It has similar symptoms to anxiety and can be triggered by a traumatic experience.

In his letters Paul never says if he is afraid of the water or not. But if he did develop a fear of the water, it would have been very natural! Still, Paul never let his bad experiences on the sea stop him from sailing again. He was determined to get to people in far-away cities to share Jesus with them, and in those days sailing was the only way to get there. So afraid or not, he did it. Even if he felt anxiety on the boat, he didn't let it stop him from talking to other people, praying with them, or writing letters. He might have felt nervous. He might have gotten symptoms like shaking or feeling sick or getting bad adrenaline rushes. But if he did, he let those things happen, and then kept going. He accepted his weaknesses and still kept doing the right thing.

In his first letter to the Corinthians, Paul tells us that our bodies are temples of the Holy Spirit (1 Corinthians 6:19). That means that in Baptism and Confirmation, the Holy Spirit comes to live in us. Wherever we go, we bring the Holy Spirit with us. No matter how weak we are, how bad we feel, or how much we are struggling, we can rely on the Holy Spirit in us to help us get through and do the right thing.

That's why nothing could stop Paul, not even his own physical or emotional weaknesses. He had them, he admitted them, he accepted them, but he didn't let them stop Jesus from acting in him. He boarded those boats even though he knew that what might happen could be really scary. He knew he wouldn't face any of it alone, and he knew that other people needed the God that he could bring them. Because he accepted himself and trusted in God, he ended up saving people's lives in that shipwreck, and changing people's lives all over the world. When we accept ourselves and trust in God, we can change people's lives too.

 ## Prayer Prompt

Lord, sometimes it's hard for me to accept my own weaknesses. I want to be strong and do everything perfectly. But you told Paul that when he was weak, you would be strong in him. Jesus, I am especially weak when _____ _____. Please be strong in me and help me to do the right thing when this happens.

 Seafarer's Challenge

Have you noticed someone in your life who also struggles with something? Try to find a way to help support and encourage them this week. Be creative and be generous!

Revelation: Golden Crowns

After this I looked, and there in heaven a door stood open! And the first voice, which I had heard speaking to me like a trumpet, said, "Come up here, and I will show you what must take place after this." At once I was in the spirit, and there in heaven stood a throne, with one seated on the throne! And the one seated there looks like jasper and carnelian, and around the throne is a rainbow that looks like an emerald. Around the throne are twenty-four thrones, and seated on the thrones are twenty-four elders, dressed in white robes, with golden crowns on their heads. Coming from the throne are flashes of lightning, and rumblings and peals of thunder, and in front of the throne burn seven flaming torches, which are the seven spirits of God; and in front of the throne there is something like a sea of glass, like crystal.

Around the throne, and on each side of the throne, are four living creatures, full of eyes in front and behind: the first living creature like a lion, the second living creature like an ox, the third living creature with a face like a human face, and the fourth living creature like a flying eagle. And the four living creatures, each of them with six wings, are full of eyes all around and inside. Day and night without ceasing they sing,

"Holy, holy, holy,
the Lord God the Almighty,
who was and is and is to come."

And whenever the living creatures give glory and honor and thanks to the one who is seated on the throne, who lives forever and ever, the twenty-four elders fall before the one who is seated on the throne and worship the one who lives forever and ever; they cast their crowns before the throne, singing,

"You are worthy, our Lord and God,
to receive glory and honor and power,
for you created all things,
and by your will they existed and were created."

Revelation 4:1–11

DAY 31
Setting Sail

This passage is pretty dramatic—with lightning and thunder and flames and a sea of glass, not to mention strange-looking creatures and elders who throw their crowns down on the ground when they sing. But this isn't just a weird story. It was written to encourage early Christians who were being persecuted. So, it can encourage us today if we read it carefully. Each strange thing in this passage represents something. For example, the elders throwing their crowns down in front of the throne represent something. The lightning and the glassy sea can tell us something too.

If you are a king or queen, you only take your crown off and put it at someone else's feet to show that they are the REAL ruler, not you. These elders are putting their crowns down to show us something. During their lives on earth, God let them in on the secret of his heart, and they discovered how much he loved them. Now, they are showing us that even though they were leaders, they were always leading the way to this person that they loved—to the one God who created them, loved them, and brought them to be with him forever. They are letting us in on the secret of God's heart and inviting us to get to know that heart better.

And in case we don't understand just how much love God has in his heart for us, John shows us the lightning and glassy sea as an example.

FACT: Sometimes lightning strikes the sand on a beach. If the lightning is hot enough, and if the sand on the beach has enough quartz or silica in it, it can create a streak of glass called a fulgur-

> ite. Fulgurites are usually in the shape of a short tube and are very breakable. They are rare to find, but if you can find one it's like holding frozen lightning in your hand!

Lightning is a beautiful, powerful thing from above. In a way, it is too beautiful and powerful, because if it hit us, we could die! But God wants us to be able to hold and treasure what is good and beautiful. He does let us touch lightning by bringing it down to earth and giving it an earthly shape in fulgurites. While these are very rare, a few lucky people really do get to hold and treasure lightning in their hands.

God is beautiful and powerful too—way too beautiful and powerful for us! But he lets us touch him. When God sent his only Son, Jesus, into the world, Jesus took on an earthly body. He let us touch him. But in this case, that amazing privilege isn't just for the lucky few who were alive when he walked the earth. Even now, as we wait for Jesus to come again, he still lets us touch him every time we receive him in the Eucharist. When we receive the Eucharist on our tongue or in our hands, we are holding and treasuring the most important and loving person in the entire universe. When we receive the Eucharist, God lets us in on the secret of his humble, loving, and generous heart. And like the elders who throw down their crowns, we have the joy of getting to show other people the loving heart of their real and only King.

Prayer Prompt

Lord, you are my only King. Thank you for letting me in on your heart, for loving me, and for letting me touch you. I want other people to know you. Help me to show other people what kind of King you are, what kind of heart you have, and how much you love them. Help me to invite them to get to know you too.

 ## Seafarer's Challenge

The next time you receive the Eucharist, remember that God is literally letting you touch him. How do you want that to change the way you receive him? How do you want holding him inside of you to change how you leave the church building? Make a goal for yourself of how you want to receive the Eucharist with more reverence from now on.

DAY 32

Deep Dive

The Book of Revelation was written by a follower of Jesus named John—possibly the apostle John himself. It is a pretty mysterious book. It is written in a style that uses a lot of images. Some parts are meant to be a riddle for us to hold in our hearts, and other parts are meant to be very clear. This passage is a bit of both.

We see twenty-four elders, or leaders of the Church, around the throne of the Lord. In front of the throne is what John calls "something like a sea of glass, like crystal." This is very interesting because, even if John didn't know it, the sea can actually create some types of glass.

FACT: Submarine volcanoes are volcanoes that are under the sea. When they are active, they erupt magma from below the earth's crust up into the water. The cold water makes the magma cool down much faster than it would on land, and that causes the magma to solidify into different forms, including volcanic glass. There are many different types of volcanic glass, each with a different name. Volcanic glass doesn't look like the glass in your window—it has color and isn't as see-through. Volcanic glass can range from white to black, gold to brown, or blue to green. You can find volcanic glass in areas that were underwater thousands or millions of years ago with volcanic activity, from Canada to

Russia, Hawaii to Iceland, Ethiopia to Australia. When you find formations of volcanic glass, you know that there was a submarine volcano there once.

Each Christian is called to be like a submarine volcano. A submarine volcano provides an opening to the hot magma near the heart of the earth, becoming a channel of that magma into the water. When the magma meets the water, it creates something beautiful. Even after the volcano goes extinct, we can tell it was there once because of the beautiful volcanic glass it left behind. As Christians, if we are open to the warmth of God's love, we become a channel of this love from the heart of Christ out into the world around us. When that love meets the world, it can transform people and situations into something more beautiful. And even after we are gone, people can tell from the good that we leave behind that a Christian was here.

What kind of legacy do you want to leave behind you? What do you want people to remember about you when you go to see God face-to-face? What is one thing about Jesus Christ that you hope people will get to know by how you channel his love into the world?

Prayer Prompt

Lord Jesus, thank you for the gift of my life. I know that one day I will get to see you face-to-face. When I do, I hope I can leave behind me a legacy that reminds people of you. Help me to channel your love and mercy to the people and situations around me. I trust you to make them something beautiful.

Sailor's Log

Write or draw something about Jesus that you want other people to learn about from the way you live your life.

Part Three

THE CHURCH

Life is like a voyage on the sea . . . often dark and stormy . . . in which we watch for the stars that indicate the route. The true stars of our life are the people who have lived good lives. They are lights of hope. Certainly, Jesus Christ is the true light, the sun that has risen above all the shadows. . . . But to reach him we also need lights close by—people who shine with his light and so guide us along our way.

—Pope Benedict XVI, *Spe Salvi*

God hasn't finished writing this story. His living word transforms the lives of those who listen to it, from biblical times right up to today.

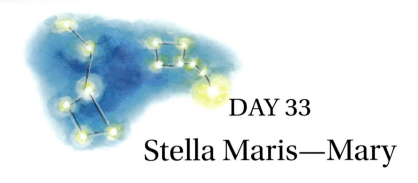

DAY 33

Stella Maris—Mary

A great portent appeared in heaven: a woman clothed with the sun, with the moon under her feet, and on her head a crown of twelve stars.

Revelation 12:1

When sailors sail the sea, it's essential that they keep their ship sailing in the right direction. Near home, sailors can recognize familiar coastlines or islands to tell them where they are. But out of sight of land, unless sailors have modern equipment they have to turn their attention to the sky. During the day, the sun helps sailors know their direction, because the sun rises in the east and sets in the west. But at night, that helper fades into the darkness. There is nothing to help people steer in the right direction . . . except a lodestar.

> **FACT**: A lodestar is a star used for navigation. The most common lodestar in the northern hemisphere is the north star, called "Polaris." Amazingly, even though all the other stars in the night sky shift positions as the earth rotates, Polaris always stays in the same spot because it shines directly over the north pole, the axis on which the earth rotates. A sailor who can find Polaris knows which way is north. Polaris is easy to find because it's in a constellation: the last star on the tail of the Little Bear (Ursa Minor), also known as the Little Dipper.

"Stella Maris" means "Star of the Sea" in Latin. It's one of the most ancient titles for Mary. We call her "Stella Maris" because she is our lodestar in our journey toward meeting God face-to-face in heaven. When things are clear and easy, following Jesus seems straightforward. But when things get difficult and confusing, sometimes we can't see Jesus anymore, and we get disoriented. We want to follow Jesus, but we can't figure out how.

In times like these, we can look to Mary. Mary shows us what it means to follow Jesus. She shows us how to be open and faithful to God when things are confusing or difficult. And she prays for us too. We can even ask her to help us to listen to the Holy Spirit, because she knows how to listen and love bravely. Mary's example and her prayers always help us to find our way back to Jesus. Mary is our lodestar in the dark night of our lives.

 Prayer Prompt

Lord Jesus, thank you for the gift of your mother, Mary, as an example of how to follow you, and as a mother who prays for me. Mary, thank you for everything you did to be open to God. Stay with me when it feels like everything is dark, and I don't know where God is. Help me to listen to the Holy Spirit, to follow your son Jesus in everything, and to love the Father with all my heart like you did.

Hail Mary, full of grace, the Lord is with thee. Blessed art thou among women, and blessed is the fruit of thy womb, Jesus. Holy Mary, mother of God, pray for us sinners, now and at the hour of our death. Amen.

Seafarer's Challenge

When you are brave, you are being like Mary. The first joyful mystery of the Rosary, the Annunciation, is straight from the Gospel of Luke 1:26–38. Read over how Mary responded when God asked her to do something that seemed impossible. Pray one decade of the Rosary with this mystery, asking for trust and courage like Mary's. Draw what you think this scene might have looked like in real life.

DAY 34

Saint Brendan

"Where were you when I laid the foundation of the earth?
    Tell me, if you have understanding.
Who determined its measurements—surely you know!
    Or who stretched the line upon it?
On what were its bases sunk,
    or who laid its cornerstone
when the morning stars sang together
    and all the heavenly beings shouted for joy?

"Or who shut in the sea with doors
    when it burst out from the womb?—
when I made the clouds its garment,
    and thick darkness its swaddling band,
and prescribed bounds for it,
    and set bars and doors,
and said, 'Thus far shall you come, and no farther,
    and here shall your proud waves be stopped'?"

Job 38:4–11

Brendan was an Irish monk with big dreams, who lived shortly after the time of Saint Patrick. One day, Brendan heard something strange from a traveler. The traveler told Brendan about a voyage he had made by sailing far west. Rather than falling off the edge of the world, as some sailors thought might happen, the traveler had found the "Promised Land of the Saints," a land that had been there since the world was created.

Brendan was fascinated. He decided to take fourteen of his fellow monks to see if they could reach this land. They set sail in a leather boat. Some probably doubted that they would return.

Brendan and his crew were at sea looking for the "Promised Land of the Saints" for a long time, much longer than they thought it should take. At one point, the monks spotted a small bare island ahead. They made their way over to it, pulled their boat up, and stepped ashore. But when the island started to move, they realized it wasn't an island at all—they were on top of a whale that was sunning itself! They scrambled back into the boat just in time, and the whale submerged.

Eventually, the monks did find the "Promised Land of the Saints." A mysterious man met them there, saying that they had taken so long to arrive because God had wanted them to discover many things on their journey. After staying a few days, the monks sailed back to Ireland, which was a much quicker trip because of the prevailing west wind behind them. Scientists and historians debated for a long time how far Brendan had gone to reach this land. Some suggested he might have discovered Newfoundland, the easternmost province of Canada. Others said it was impossible for Irish boats to sail that far way back then.

FACT: In 1977, a British explorer named Tim Severin decided to find out, once and for all, if Saint Brendan could have actually made it to Newfoundland. He built a boat exactly like what the Irish monks would have had in the late 400s or early 500s and used the accounts of Brendan's voyage to direct his course, setting sail from Ireland. Defying all the odds, they made it to Newfoundland! Tim Severin wrote a book about his adventure, called *The Brendan Voyage*.

Brendan and his fellow monks planned their quest carefully. They estimated how far the "Promised Land of the Saints" might be, packing food and water rations accordingly. But nothing went according to plan. The journey took much longer, and they probably worried about running out of food and water. But God had a bigger dream for them. He used their journey to help them discover unknown islands and meet new people. In the end, Brendan and the monks learned that the world was bigger and more diverse than they ever imagined. When they returned to Ireland, they were more in love with God than ever before.

Sometimes things are like this for us. We want something to turn out a certain way and we do everything we can to make sure it goes according to plan, but then things get more complicated than we thought they would be. Sometimes as God did with Brendan, he redirects our route because he wants to show us something even more amazing than what we were aiming for. His dreams for us are so much bigger and more amazing than our dreams for ourselves!

Prayer Prompt

Take some quiet time to tell God about your dreams. What things do you want to do? What adventures do you want to have? Then ask him to show you his dreams for you. Maybe, as with Brendan, God will take the dreams you already have and blow them out of the water! Or maybe he will surprise you with new dreams. Remember, he might not show you right away. But keep watching out for his answers. And make sure to thank him when you find out what they are!

Sailor's Log

When Brendan and his crew landed on a whale thinking it was an island, they probably realized that God has a sense of humour! Draw a picture or write a poem about this kerfuffle that brings out the humour in it. If you feel comfortable, share the funny story with your friends or family.

DAY 35

Saint Francis Xavier

. . . all your waves and your billows
have gone over me.

Psalm 42:7

When you pass through the waters, I will be with you . . .

Isaiah 43:2

Francis Xavier had no idea who his university roommates would be, or that they would all become saints! Francis wanted to become rich and powerful, so he was very annoyed when his roommate, Ignatius of Loyola, kept talking about living for God. When his other roommate, Peter Faber, started listening to Ignatius, Francis was extra frustrated. But after a while, Ignatius asked Francis to take a good look at the deepest desires of his heart. Francis ended up realizing that he did yearn to live for a loving God, and that God had been waiting for his love for a long time.

Ignatius, Peter, and Francis started the Jesuit missionaries to spread the love of Jesus to people who had never met him. When they took their vows, they were each given a crucifix. It became their most precious possession because it was the symbol of everything Christ had done for them and everything they had promised to do for Christ. When Francis left home to bring the Gospel to Asia, he brought his crucifix with him as a sign of the life that he and Jesus would share forever.

Sailing to Asia was dangerous. Francis knew this, but his heart ached for the people of Asia who had never met the God who loved them so much. He knew that his heart ached like that because Jesus' heart ached about it too, and Jesus was sharing this with him. So he went, trusting in Jesus to do whatever was best.

A terrible storm hit. It was too strong for their ship. Even the best sailors knew they were about to drown. That's when Francis did something crazy—he pulled out his precious crucifix, asked God to spare their lives, and hurled his crucifix overboard into the sea.

The storm weakened, and they hit land. The sailors and passengers sat on the shore, trembling, feeling sick, trying to catch their breath, realizing they were still alive.

Just then, a crab came up out of the ocean, dragging Francis' crucifix behind it.

> **FACT**: In hurricanes at sea, high waves mix warm surface waters with colder water below, causing rough undercurrents. These undercurrents, which change the flow and temperature of the water, can reach to 300 feet below the surface, endangering shellfish and other creatures that cannot quickly swim out of the stormy area.

Francis was young and strong, but in that storm, he realized that staying alive wasn't in his control. But God was in control. Francis knew that if God was calling him home to heaven, then he would go. He also knew that if God still had work for him, he could trust that God would get him ashore to do it.

We can't control everything in life. Sometimes that's scary. But we can trust God to work through bad things that happen to bring about good. Francis Xavier trusted God to do what was best, whether it was bringing him home to meet Jesus face to face, or going to Asia to teach others about Jesus. When he prayed for God to save them, he trusted that no matter what, God would do what was best. He threw his crucifix into the ocean as a sign that he trusted God with everything precious to him. And God sent the crucifix back to remind Francis that he was precious to him too.

Have you ever heard of an "Act of Surrender"? It's a prayer that helps us to trust God with everything precious to us. It's like what Francis Xavier did in the storm, but in words. Think of things you are trying to control in your life and entrust them to God. After all, he cares about your life even more than you do!

Prayer Prompt

Act of Surrender today: My God, I do not know what will happen to me today. I only know that whatever happens to me you can use for my good. This is enough for me. I adore your eternal plans and your promise of love to me. I accept these with all my heart for love of you. I offer you my whole self, and join my offering to that of Jesus, my divine Savior. In Jesus' name, I ask you for patience and acceptance of your will for me. Thank you for being faithful in everything.

Seafarer's Challenge

Set up a crucifix in your room to remind you of Christ's love for you. When there are things troubling you, place your concerns beneath the cross to show Jesus you trust him even with these things. Got a math test? After you study, put your notes beneath the crucifix before you go to bed. Family fighting? Place a family photo under the crucifix. Struggling to feel like you fit in, or that you matter? Sit beneath the crucifix for a little bit, entrusting the gift of who you are to Jesus.

DAY 36
Saint Lorenzo Ruiz

O Lord, you have searched me and known me.
You know when I sit down and when I rise up;
    you discern my thoughts from far away.
You search out my path . . .
    and are acquainted with all my ways . . .

Where can I go from your spirit?
    Or where can I flee from your presence? . . .
If I take the wings of the morning
    and settle at the farthest limits of the sea,
even there your hand shall lead me,
    and your right hand shall hold me fast. . . .

For it was you who formed my inward parts;
    you knit me together in my mother's womb.
I praise you, for I am fearfully and wonderfully made.
    Wonderful are your works;
that I know very well. . . .
Your eyes beheld my unformed substance.
In your book were written
    all the days that were formed for me,
    when none of them as yet existed.
How weighty to me are your thoughts, O God!

> How vast is the sum of them!
> I try to count them—they are more than the sand;
> I come to the end—I am still with you.
>
> Psalm 139:1–3, 7, 9–10, 13–14, 16–18

Lorenzo Ruiz was born in the Philippines to a Chinese father and a Filipino mother. He was an altar-server as a child, and as a young man he joined a prayer group. After he married, he and his wife had three kids. His little family lived a quiet life.

But everything changed when Lorenzo was accused of murder.

They said he killed a Spaniard. It seems like a false accusation, although we don't have evidence of whether he was innocent or guilty. Either way, Lorenzo didn't stick around. He ran to the only safe place he knew—a boat.

> **FACT**: People have escaped life-threatening situations by boat for thousands of years. Today, migrants and refugees risk their lives by boarding unreliable boats to reach the shores of a safer country. Some make the news, like refugees trying to escape from Cuba to America in the late 1900s, or refugees from Africa and the Middle East trying to escape to Europe in the 2000s. Many of these boats make it to the shores of another country, but many others are lost at sea.

Lorenzo found a ship sailing to Japan with some European and Japanese priests. He asked them for refuge, and they agreed to take Lorenzo with them. Sailing was slow, and they spent many days on the open sea.

This gave Lorenzo a lot of time to think. He was running away to save his freedom and his life . . . but what did it mean to really be free? What did it mean to live your life to the full? At sea, Lorenzo had time to pray about all this. He had time to sit with his God, whom he couldn't run away from, who was with him always, who knew him through and through, and who loved him more than anyone else. Lorenzo had time to understand that real freedom and lasting life come only from God's love.

When they reached Japan, they discovered that the government had started persecuting Christians. They were all arrested and accused of the crime of being Christian.

Lorenzo had just run from being accused of one crime right into being accused of another. The Japanese officials gave him the chance to run again. All Lorenzo had to do was publicly give up his faith in God, and he could be free. But Lorenzo knew that walking away without Jesus was not freedom. This time, Lorenzo refused to run away. He chose to be loyal to Jesus, even if it meant death.

Lorenzo was found guilty of being Christian, tortured, and killed. But he had found true freedom in the heart of God, who knew him better than anyone else, and who loved him more than life itself. His last words were: "I . . . wholeheartedly accept death for God. If I had a thousand lives, I would offer them all to him."

Are there important things in your life that you have tried to ignore, hide, or run from? In those times did you have a chance to pray to see where God was? Take some time today to just sit with God and ask him the questions that are on your heart. Let him give you the strength to face anything difficult happening in your life.

Prayer Prompt

Lord, there are some things that I just want to run away from. Sometimes I even want to run away from you. But I know that you already know and love me more than I can imagine. Help me to be open and honest with you, to rely on you, and to trust you. Give me the courage to face situations that I need to face and to leave situations that I need to leave.

Sailor's Log

Draw or write about a situation that makes you want to run and hide. Then at night, put your description of this situation underneath a crucifix or image of Jesus in your room while you sleep. If you don't have a crucifix or picture of Jesus in your room yet, you can draw one yourself or print one out. Trust that he will give you the courage to face whatever you need to do in that situation.

DAY 37

Saint Marguerite Bourgeoys

> The purpose in a man's heart is like deep water,
> but a man of understanding will draw it out.
>
> Proverbs 20:5 (ESV)

Marguerite Bourgeoys was an unusual woman for her time. She didn't get married as people expected her to. Instead, she left her home in France to make the risky crossing of the Atlantic and start a teaching order of religious sisters in the dangerous New France (now Quebec, Canada).

When Marguerite boarded the ship to New France, people thought she was crazy. She was one of the only women aboard, and she didn't bring anyone from home with her. Why was she risking her safety to make this crossing alone? Why was she throwing her life away by going to a struggling New France when she could be living comfortably in familiar France? Why was she trying to found a new teaching order of sisters instead of joining a cloister to live a quiet life? People on board decided Marguerite must have a bad personality, otherwise she would have been able to be content with what God made available to her at home in France.

But that wasn't true. Marguerite was going to New France because she heard God calling her to care for his beloved children there who were suffering, with no one to help them. She was nervous, because she knew it would be hard and she was alone. But she trusted that since God was asking her to do this, he would give her all the grace she needed to do it.

Partway into their journey across the Atlantic, an epidemic broke out on board their ship.

> **FACT**: Ships have a bad track record for bringing harmful diseases or animals to new lands. Germs or wildlife from one continent can accidentally get onto a ship and survive the trip across the ocean, harming people or habitats in a new continent. Quarantining passengers before they come ashore and checking ships for hidden wildlife are measures that can still be used today.

This ship had picked up harmful germs from the trip it had made before this one. Marguerite became an unofficial nurse overnight. She sat with sick passengers and took care of them. She talked to patients who were lonely and afraid. When some passengers got so sick that they were going to die, she stayed to pray with them until they were ready to go home to God.

After that, no one questioned Marguerite's reasons for going to New France. They learned from experience that she made every decision in her life based on the love and mercy of God's heart.

When Marguerite arrived in New France, everyone came to respect her heart. She opened schools for children who could not pay for an education, including one in a Haudenosaunee (Iroquois) village. Her heart knew no boundaries—no matter where people came from, or whether they liked her or not, she held out to them the loving hand of God, just as she had on her first trip across the ocean.

Marguerite crossed the Atlantic Ocean seven times, adding up to a total of one year of her life spent at sea.

We can have lots of reasons for doing things. Sometimes our reasons are selfish, sometimes they are good, and sometimes they are a little bit of both. Think back over the decisions you made this week. How many were really motivated by wanting to share God's truth, mercy, or love?

Prayer Prompt

Lord, sometimes I do things for the wrong reasons. You know my reasons even before I do. Please forgive me for the times that I let selfish reasons decide my actions. Help me to make my decisions more thoughtfully, bringing you into each one.

Sailor's Log

Make a list of all the good reasons you made decisions this week. Are there other things you want to help guide your decisions next week? Add them to your list.

DAY 38

Saint Damien of Molokai

Therefore confess your sins to one another, and pray for one another, so that you may be healed. The prayer of the righteous is powerful and effective.

James 5:16

You will cast all our sins
   into the depths of the sea.

Micah 7:19

Father Damien was a priest from Belgium who sailed to Hawaii as a missionary. He volunteered to go to a leper colony on the island of Molokai. People who contracted leprosy in Hawaii were sent to live on Molokai so they wouldn't contaminate anyone else—a permanent quarantine. They were separated from everyone they knew and loved, without medical or other help because people were so afraid of catching the disease. But Father Damien wasn't afraid. He knew these people needed God, and so he went.

> **FACT**: Scurvy was a disease, caused by a deficiency in vitamin C, that afflicted many sailors. It caused some crazy symptoms, such as teeth falling out! British sailors became known as "Limeys"

because they began eating limes on board to prevent scurvy. Scurvy was dangerous, but it wasn't contagious. However, many contagious diseases did cross water barriers with sailors and spread like wildfire in communities that had no immunity. People had lived through epidemics of contagious diseases and knew how catastrophic contagion could be. This made fear of diseases like leprosy greater.

Even though Father Damien was a brave and loving man, he made mistakes and sinned like anyone else. But on Molokai, there were no other priests to hear his confession. Finally, after he had been on the island over a year, a ship came to deliver supplies with a priest on board. But the priest was not allowed to come ashore, and Father Damien couldn't board the ship because he might be contagious. Father Damien had a choice—he could stay on the island and miss going to confession, or he could row out beside the boat and shout his confession up to the priest on deck, knowing that all the sailors would hear him too.

Father Damien decided that the grace of God was more important than the embarrassment of sailors hearing his sins, so he got into a boat, rowed up to the side of the big ship, and shouted his confession to the priest standing on deck. And he received the grace he had yearned for so much.

Going to confession and apologizing to others can be awkward. But even though it's uncomfortable, it is healing—just like medicine that tastes gross but makes us better. We may not like it, but we do it because it's important. When we are brave enough to face what we have done wrong and confess it to God and to others with humble hearts, God gives us so much grace! We learn to be brave, faithful, loving, and free.

Prayer Prompt

At the end of Confession, the priest will ask you to say an "Act of Contrition." If you don't have one memorized, copy this one down to bring into Confession with you. (If you forget, just tell the priest, and he can walk you through it!)

O my God, I am heartily sorry for having offended you, and I detest all my sins because of your just punishments, but most of all because they offend you, my God, who are all good and deserving of all my love. I firmly resolve, with the help of your grace, to sin no more and to avoid the near occasions of sin. Amen.

Seafarer's Challenge

Find out where you can go to Confession this month. Before you go, make an examination of conscience (to help, you can read the Ten Commandments or look back at Moses' Deep Dive on page 33). Be honest with yourself so that you can be honest with God. After you come back from Confession, do your penance and say a thanksgiving prayer to God for the grace he has given you! And remember, if you get scared or don't want to go, ask Saint Damien of Molokai to pray that you will build up the motivation and courage to get yourself there to receive God's grace, no matter how you feel.

DAY 39

Saint Josephine Bakhita

> He heals the brokenhearted,
>   and binds up their wounds.
> He determines the number of the stars;
>   he gives to all of them their names.
>
> Psalm 147:3–4

When Bakhita stepped aboard a ship for the first time, she was leaving her homeland of the Sudan and sailing to Genoa with her "owners." Yes, Bakhita was a slave.

Kidnapped from her village as a little girl by slave traders, she had been so traumatized that she forgot her own name. The traders called her "Bakhita," which is Arabic for "fortunate" or "lucky." Bakhita was sold again and again, enduring abuse and trauma, until she was finally sold to an Italian family living in Africa. The Italian family treated her well, although they had no intention of setting her free. They made her the nanny of their little girl. When the family decided to return to Italy, they brought Bakhita with them.

Bakhita's village had not been Christian, so she had never learned about the one God—Father, Son, and Holy Spirit. She didn't encounter him through any of her abusive "owners" either. But even in the midst of trauma, Bakhita could spot beauty. She was a curious child who became a wise young woman. She knew that real, lasting beauty could only come from goodness and love. While she did not encounter much beauty in her life as a slave, she did find it in nature. She once said: "I remembered looking at the moon and stars and the beautiful things in nature and saying to myself, 'Who is the master of all these beautiful things?' And I experienced a great desire to see him and know him and honor him."

At sea, Bakhita would have had the opportunity to discover the beauty of the sky in a very unique way.

> **FACT**: Today, there are special night cruises just for stargazing! Passengers sail out at night to experience the night sky free of any light pollution or visual barriers to see things that you would never be able to see from land. Depending on what hemisphere the cruise sails in, passengers can see the full band of the Milky Way, the northern lights, colorful nebulas, or even the Andromeda Galaxy from over two million light years away!

After her sea crossing, Bakhita lived in Italy. She started to learn about Christianity. When her "owners" had to leave on a long trip, Bakhita was delighted to be enrolled in a boarding school run by Canossian sisters. It was with these sisters that Bakhita finally got to know the Master of the stars whom she had wondered about for so long, the one who made things so beautiful that she knew he was all goodness. For the first time, she encountered a Master who frees.

Bakhita knew what she had to do. She bravely stood up to her "owners" to demand her freedom. The Canossian sisters and the local bishop backed her up. The first thing she did as a free woman was to be baptized, taking the name Josephine. She entered the same order of sisters that had taught her about Jesus, where she dedicated her whole life to loving, and being loved by, Jesus.

For a long time, Josephine Bakhita had not had people in her life who could help her grow into a relationship with God. But God had revealed himself to her anyway. He had reached out to her through beauty, especially the beauty of nature. In nature, God touches us, delights us, fascinates us, meets us, and heals us in a very special way.

What is something about nature that God uses to uplift and inspire your spirit? What does this teach you about who God is and how he reaches out to you?

Prayer Prompt

Take a moment to thank God for the parts of nature that touch you the most. Ask him to keep teaching you more of who he is through this.

Seafarer's Challenge

Bring one cool element of nature inside to help you pray and worship God from the quiet of your room. It could be the sketch of a leaf, a star chart, an interesting rock, a little cactus . . . anything that will help you pray in your room without making too much of a mess.

DAY 40

My Story
(write your name in the blank)

It's been 39 days, and you've read how God can reveal himself on the sea, in the Old Testament, in the New Testament, and in the lives of people who continue to love him. But the story doesn't stop with other people. The story continues with you. It's your turn. This is your chapter.

By now, you've walked through many of the big sea stories of the Bible and some other Scripture verses as well. For your Scripture verse, choose a story or verse that made a big impression on you or that you related to the most. It can be one you prayed with in this devotional or a different one that you found in the Bible. Write it here:

Read over what you just wrote and think about it. Why does this strike you so much? What does it mean to you? How does it relate to your life? What is God revealing to you about himself? Write your reflection on this Scripture passage here:

....

....

....

....

....

Is there a cool fact about the sea, the Bible, or your life that helps you dive deeper into understanding God's message to you in this Scripture passage? Write it here:

....

....

....

....

....

Write a prayer, speaking to God about this Scripture passage or about your life. When we write our prayers, it's like writing a little note to God. He reads each word:

....

....

....

....

....

What is one thing that this Scripture passage inspires you to say or do? Make your own Sailor's Log or Seafarer's Challenge here:

....

....

....

....

....

Safe at Port

Dear Reader,

You have come to the end of this voyage, but your journey is far from over. The Lord has many adventures in store for you on the seas of your life. Now that you've prayed through this devotional once, you can go back to the stories, illustrations, and reflections that really had an impact on you. You can pray with any part as many times as the Holy Spirit inspires you to. After all, Scripture is the living word of God—you can always dive deeper!

Explore a Bible. Pick one up and start reading the Gospel of Matthew. In the Gospels, God will speak to you not just from the sea, but also from deserts and gardens, caves and mountain tops. And each time you pray, he will whisper life into the silence of your own beating heart.

May your adventures with the Lord be many!

> "Our heart needs to be larger than the seas and the oceans. Love each other as children of God, brothers and sisters, companions on the road to heaven."
>
> —*Blessed James Alberione*

How to Look Up a Passage in the Bible

When you see letters and numbers that look like this: **Jn 3:16**, it's what we call a Bible citation. A Bible citation tells you how to find a certain passage in the Bible. While you can always type a citation in your Internet browser to find the exact text, it's important to know how to find it in the Bible itself, especially if you want to see what came before and after that exact passage. Here's how to look it up in an actual Bible:

— The first part of the citation, "Jn," refers to the "book" of the Bible. The Bible is really a collection of seventy-three short books printed together in one big book. Sometimes in a citation the name of the book is written out (John), but often it is abbreviated (Jn). In the front of your Bible, you can find a list of the books and their abbreviations, as well as a table of contents.

— The next part, the first number ("3"), refers to the chapter of the book.

— The part after the colon ("16") refers to the verse of the chapter. In some Bibles, the verse numbers are printed (in very tiny type) in the text itself; in other Bibles, the verse numbers run alongside the text, in the margin.

— So to find Jn 3:16, you would go to the Gospel according to John, turn to chapter 3, and find verse 16: "For God so loved the world that he gave his only Son, so that everyone who believes in him may not perish but may have eternal life."

How Catholics Understand the Bible

It's helpful to look at the way Catholics understand the meaning of the Bible. Catholics understand that every line of Scripture can have several layers of meaning. We can speak of the **intended meaning** and various kinds of **spiritual meanings**.

When reading the Bible, the first thing we do as Catholics is look at the **intended meaning**, what the author of a particular passage intended to say. So, for example, in the passage where Moses parts the Red Sea, the intended meaning is that through Moses, God saved the Jewish People from slavery. He did this by means of a miracle that allowed them to escape from the Egyptian army.

Sometimes, as in this case, it's easy to understand the intended meaning. But sometimes what the words seem to say at face value is not what the author meant. When the words were first written, it might have been clear what was meant, but that was thousands of years ago and in a culture very different than ours.

Think about how your mom might say, "I have a million things to do this weekend." People who hear that understand her intended meaning: that she's feeling overwhelmed with lots of things that need to be done. We understand she doesn't intend to say she actually has 1,000,000 tasks on her to-do list. However, someone in another culture many years from now might not immediately understand the meaning of this sentence as the speaker intended. Similarly, when we try to understand what the author of a Bible passage intended to communicate, we sometimes need Scriptural experts to help explain it.

The **spiritual meaning** refers to how the things that are happening in a passage can point to other realities in our lives and the life of the Church.

Here are three different ways a passage might have a spiritual meaning. (It can have some or all of these meanings, and more than one of each!)

— It might have an **allegorical meaning**. That means that what is happening in a passage might have an even deeper meaning in Jesus. For example, the liberation from slavery by crossing the Red Sea points to or foreshadows the freedom from sin that we have when we pass through the water of Baptism. Moses' story lays the groundwork for an even deeper story that Jesus fulfills in giving us the sacrament of Baptism!

— It might have a **moral meaning**. That means that what is happening in a passage can teach us how we can live and act in a good, honest, and loving way. For example, Moses and his people were not able to fight the Egyptians in order to escape. They had to trust God and follow his instructions. This can teach us that we need God's help to break away from sin; we need to grow in love and trust of him.

— It might have an **anagogical meaning**. That means that what is happening in a passage might point to an eternal reality in heaven, helping us draw closer to God. For example, the Jewish People crossing the Red Sea on their way to the Promised Land makes us think of how crossing the water of Baptism is part of our journey to the promised land of heaven.

That's a lot of potential meaning hiding in the Bible! Thankfully, we don't have to try to figure it all out on our own or argue with other people about our own interpretations. Guided by the Holy Spirit, the Church helps us to understand all the types of meaning of Scripture based on Tradition, prayer, scholarship, and research.

Prayers Before Reading the Bible

Prayer of Faith

Lord Jesus, you came and made the blind see, the deaf hear, the mute speak, the lame walk, and the prisoners free! As I read your word, help me to see what you need me to see, to hear what I most need to hear, to speak with you honestly, to walk in your footsteps, and to be freed from anything holding me back from you!

Traditional Prayer Before Reading Scripture

Father, anoint me with your Holy Spirit,
so that as I read your eternal word,
your word may penetrate my whole being and transform me.

Grant me the blessing to be a faithful disciple
in believing the Word of God and that
I may be a light shining upon all who are in darkness. Amen.

Psalm Verse to Pray Before Reading Scripture

"Your word is a lamp to my feet, and a light to my path."

Psalm 119:105

For Further Exploration

DAY 1

You can read the second account of creation in **Genesis 2:5–25**.

DAY 4

Read an early account of a Baptism by the deacon Philip in **Acts of the Apostles 8:26–40**.

DAY 5

This was how the Lord began to show his people that he was not a God who demanded child sacrifice. He started to teach his people this by stopping Abraham and Isaac from engaging in this practice and showing them how much he valued their lives and their love. But he didn't stop there. With so many cultures at the time practicing child sacrifice, God kept deepening his people's understanding of the importance of honoring life by giving them the Ten Commandments, and through the teachings of his prophets.

You can find more about this in these passages: **Jeremiah 7:30–31** and **Deuteronomy 12:29–31**.

DAY 7

Psalm 27 is a good psalm to pray during a time of waiting for the Lord.

DAY 8

To read more about Pharaoh's choice to harden his heart to the cry of God's people and the request of God, you can read **Exodus 8:15** and **Exodus 8:32**.

DAY 13

When you read the story of these three young men, you will see that in some places their names are given as "Shadrach, Meshach, and Abednego." Those are the Babylonian names they were given in their captivity in Babylon. Their Jewish names were Hananiah, Azariah, and Mishael.

DAY 15

John 1:29–42 tells the story of how Andrew heard John the Baptist talking about Jesus.

DAY 17

Understanding all the different parts of Scripture can seem confusing or overwhelming. But there are lots of good places for us to go for help! The tradition and teaching of the Church, informed by ancient knowledge as well as modern scholarship, can help us to understand what certain parts of the Bible are talking about. Even the *Catechism of the Catholic Church* has a lot of helpful explanations about the Bible and how we can live it out today.

DAY 20

You can read about other times Jesus went alone to pray. For example, see Luke 6:12–13 (Jesus prayed the night before a big decision); Mark 1:35 (when his days were very busy, Jesus got up early to pray); and Matthew 26:36–39 (Jesus prays alone with only his three closest disciples as he prepares for his Passion).

DAY 26

If you are reading from a physical Bible, you might see little letters, numbers, and symbols scattered through the text, in addition to the verse numbers. These little characters refer to footnotes and cross references. Each publisher has a different system to connect the place in the text to the footnote or cross reference. Footnotes might be indicated by a letter, number, or an asterisk (*), and then if you look at the bottom of the page, you will see those same letters (or numbers, or the verse numbers) with little notes beside them. If cross references are included, they might be done in a similar way. Or the cross reference might be in the margin next to the related passage. You can find an explanation of the system your particular Bible uses by looking at the table of contents.

Footnotes

Footnotes might define a word for you (for example, explaining what a "Pharisee" is). They might give historical or cultural context (such as explaining how Jewish people in AD 30 felt about tax collectors and why). Or they might give alternative translations of the word from the original Hebrew or Greek.

In addition to the footnotes, some study Bibles contain notes in other parts of the Bible, such as before each book, or in the back of the Bible. Notes can be very helpful in understanding our Bibles! But it is important to remember that notes are not part of the Bible, and that means that they aren't divinely inspired. They can help you, but they aren't the word of God.

Cross References

Cross references connect the passage you are reading with another part of the Bible. It might be that an earlier passage is quoted in a later one. Or the cross reference could point to another place (especially in the Gospels) where the same story is recounted. (This is also called a "parallel passage.")

In the Bible, there are a lot of connected passages! In Biblical times, many Jewish people knew their Scripture by heart so they didn't have to say what they were quoting—everybody could tell. Today we might not be as good at recognizing them, but knowing when one passage is quoting or referring to another can help us understand much more deeply what God is saying to us.

For example: Did you know that when Jesus was dying on the Cross and gasped out the words "My God, my God, why have you forsaken me?" he was actually quoting a psalm? That line is the very first verse of Psalm 22. And if you know to follow that reference and read Psalm 22, you will see that the psalm begins in suffering, but ends in triumph, joy, and life! So when Jesus said that, he wasn't just expressing his own pain; he was also declaring the promise of what was to come!

DAY 27

To read about what Jesus' disciples did when he was arrested, tried, and crucified, check out **John 18 and 19**.

DAY 28

To read the story of Peter following Jesus after his arrest, and everything that happened, check out **Luke 22:54–62**.

DAY 31

Tips for receiving the Eucharist with reverence:

The Church asks us to fast (eat or drink nothing except water) for one hour before Holy Communion. You should also avoid chewing gum.

Try to focus on Jesus as you go up to receive Communion instead of looking around at what others are doing.

When you move toward the minister of Communion, approach with care and respect, and bow before you receive Communion. Jesus is allowing you a special moment to touch him, as your closest friend and as King of the entire universe, veiled in the form of bread and wine! It's a deeply sacred and personal moment.

If receiving on the tongue, make sure your mouth is open and your tongue extended enough that the priest can place the Host on your tongue without the risk of it falling. If receiving in the hand, put one hand (palm up) on top of the other, and cup your hands a little to make a throne for Jesus. Once the Host is placed in your hand, step aside. Don't just pick the Host up from your palm and pop it into your mouth like a snack. Place him reverently in your mouth, and then check your hands to make sure there are no particles of the Host left behind. If there are, make sure to consume those too—Jesus is present in them.

After receiving Communion, take a few moments to talk to Jesus. Thank him for being with you in such a close and personal way.

When you leave Mass, Jesus is inside you. You are bearing Jesus with you, like a walking tabernacle! Ask Jesus to help you carry him intentionally to all the places and people you will encounter in the next few hours.

About the Author

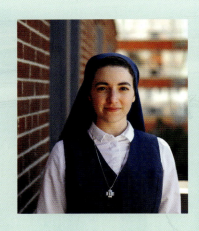

Orianne Pietra René Dyck Orianne Pietra René Dyck is a religious sister with the Daughters of St. Paul. Born in Winnipeg, Manitoba, and raised in the Ottawa Valley, she converted to the Catholic faith at the age of twelve. Despite being allergic to fish, she loves the sea! One of her favourite ocean memories is of stumbling upon wild sea lions teaching their baby pups how to swim off the coast of Peru. A former teacher and youth leader, Sister Orianne is passionate about helping youth discover the same Jesus who changed her life. Sister Orianne currently works in social media ministry. *Dive Deep* is her first published book.

About the Illustrator

Romi Caron is a professional illustrator who has created art for over 90 published books. She enjoys sharing her love for art by giving special art courses to students in schools in the Ottawa/Gatineau region. She was born in communist Czechoslovakia, where God "did not exist," and simply wearing a cross could mean losing the chance to study or a job. Romi had to "dive very deep," and in very dangerous waters, to discover the existence of God and her faith. Her discovery gave her the courage to cross the ocean and establish herself in Quebec, where she lives with her husband and three sons. The beautiful nature of the Gatineau region brings her everyday inspiration.

Pauline
BOOKS & MEDIA

Who are the Daughters of St. Paul?

We are Catholic sisters with a mission. Our task is to bring the love of Jesus to everyone like Saint Paul did. You can find us in over 50 countries. Our founder, Blessed James Alberione, showed us how to reach out to the world through the media. That's why we publish books, make movies and apps, record music, broadcast on radio, perform concerts, help people at our bookstores, visit parishes, use social media and the Internet, and pray for all of you.